LANGUAGE, CULTURE, ART AND POLITICS IN THE CHANGING WORLD

Editörler:
Prof. Dr. Muhlise Coşgun ÖGEYİK
Dr. Kutay UZUN

Language, Culture, Art and Politics in the Changing World

© NÜVE KÜLTÜR MERKEZİ YAYINLARI: 150
İnceleme-Araştırma Dizisi: 116

Bu kitap ve kitabın özgün özellikleri tamamen Nüve Kültür Merkezi'ne aittir. Hiçbir şekilde taklit edilemez. Yayınevinin izni olmadan kısmen ya da tamamen kopyalanamaz, çoğaltılamaz.
Nüve Kültür Merkezi hukukî sorumluluk ve takibat hakkını saklı tutar.

Mayıs 2021

Yayınevi Editörleri: **Salih TİRYAKİ – Emre Vadi BALCI**
Genel Yayın Yönetmeni: **İsmail ÇALIŞKAN**

ISBN 978-625-7606-10-3

T.C.
Kültür ve Turizm Bakanlığı
Yayıncı Sertifika No: **16195**

Kapak Tasarım:
Baskı Öncesi Hazırlık: **Mehmet ATEŞ**
meh_ates@hotmail.com

Baskı & Cilt: **Şelale Ofset**
Fevzi Çakmak Mh. Hacı Bayram Cad. No. 22 Karatay/KONYA
Tel: +90.532.159 40 91 selalemat2012@hotmail.com
KTB S. No: **46806** - Basım Tarihi: **MAYIS 2021**

KÜTÜPHANE BİLGİ KARTI
- Cataloging in Publication Data (CIP) -

ÖGEYİK / UZUN, Muhlise Coşgun / Kutay
Language, Culture, Art and Politics in the Changing World

ANAHTAR KAVRAMLAR
1. Dil, 2. Kültür, 3. Sanat, 4. Siyaset, 5. Ekonomi
- key concepts –
1. Language, 2. Culture, 3. Art, 4. Politics, 5. Economy

www.literaturkacademia.com
romantikkitap@gmail.com

/ Nkmliteraturk

M. Muzaffer Cad. Rampalı Çarşı Alt Kat No: 35-36-41
Meram / KONYA Tel: 0.332.352 23 03 Fax: 0.332.342 42 96

Ул. М. Музаффер, рынок Рампалы, нижний этаж № 35-36-41
Мерам, КОНЬЯ, тел.: +90 332 352 23 03,
факс: +90 332 342 42 96

Dağıtım: **EMEK KİTAP**
Akçaburgaz Mah. 3137. Sk. Ali Rıza Güvener İş Merkezi No: 28
Esenyurt / İSTANBUL
www.emekkitap.com - Telefaks +90 212 671 68 10

ORTA ASYA OFFICE:
Mikrareyon Kok Jar/23   Bishkek / KYRGYSZTAN
Tel: +996 700 13 50 00   -   Telefaks: + 996 552 13 50 00
ОФИС В ЦЕНТРАЛЬНОЙ АЗИИ:
Микрорайон Кок Жар/23   Бишкек / КЫРГЫЗСТАН
Тел.: +996 700 13 50 00 – Телефакс: +996 552 13 50 00

Дистрибьютор: **EMEK KİTAP**
Район Акчабургаз, ул. Али Рыза 3137, бизнес центр «Гювенер» № 28,
Эсеньюрт / СТАМБУЛ
www.emekkitap.com — Телефакс: +90 212 671 68 10

LANGUAGE, CULTURE, ART AND POLITICS IN THE CHANGING WORLD

Editörler:
Prof. Dr. Muhlise COŞGUN ÖGEYİK
Dr. Kutay UZUN

PREFACE

Life in the 21th century has already been marked by a changing world in many aspects. The Internet has reached virtually the whole world, neoliberal marketing policies have become more aggressive than ever and alternative economies such as cryptocurrencies have emerged within the first quarter of this century. Adding to the equation the ever-increasing population of the world and the much increased connectedness of its residents, novel definitions of what have already been known have emerged, reflecting the changing life in our time.

The changes to life as observed in our century has also made it explicit that the concepts we tend to define continually are far from being stable and static. Instead, the current status of the world we live in prove time and again that those changes are instable, dynamic, non-linear and coadaptive, signifying the difficulty of achieving predictability.

In a world that is best defined as dynamic and unpredictable, management becomes a key term for the harmony in life that every person tends to strive for. Efficiency in managing harmony among people, cities, industries, politics, education, arts, organizations or countries stands out as the utmost necessity regardless of the context one might be in. Without the endeavor to manage efficiently, the harmony that we all look for would become even more difficult to achieve.

Such a harmony through efficient management, perhaps naturally, necessitates the coadaptation of academic disciplines just as it does the same in other fields in life. For this reason, multidisciplinary academic studies are now more important than ever because the instable, non-linear and dynamic nature of life and its changes are highly unlikely to be explained by a single discipline in isolation. The efficient management of the planet earth undoubtedly requires the efficient coexistence of societies, industries, education, politics and countries.

All those structures forming human life in the world should coexist and academic studies are no exception to ensure a proper, scientific understanding of the worldly phenomena. In that respect, this book aims to present multidisciplinary perspectives in respect of the management of the societies, politics, arts, industries, international relations and education. We hope that the chapters within, distinguished works of the mentioned disciplines, will inform the readers regarding the interplay among various branches of science and contribute to the knowledge base of the world regarding language, culture, arts and politics in an ever-changing world.

Prof. Dr. Muhlise Coşgun Ögeyik
Dr. Kutay Uzun

CONTENTS

PREFACE 5
CONTENTS 7

Student Teachers' Perceptions of Form-Focused Instruction in Foreign Language Classes
Muhlise Coşgun ÖGEYİK 9

Emotional Load, Formality, Informativeness and Implicature in Relation to L2 Writing Performance
Kutay UZUN 19

Metropolitan Urban Management and Effects of Covid-19 Pandemic on Metropolitan City Management in Italy
Melike KAYIRAL - Mesut KAYAER 31

Gender and Climate Change
Tefide KIZILDENİZ - Cansu ÇİFTÇİ - Alea LAIDLAW 53

The Biconditionality of Art-Politics
Barış ÇAĞLAR 83

Industry 4.0 Vision to Reach The Lean- Six Sigma Targets
Mustafa BAYHAN 89

The Counter Hegemony Area of Past Extended to Present on the Axis of The Memory: Documentary Film
Seher SEYLAN 113

Feedback Strategies and E-Assessment in Online Learning
Zafer GÜNEY 135

Impact of Organizational Culture on Organizational Innovativeness: Moderating Effect of Organizational Power
Mehmet KIZILOĞLU 155

The Theory of Idealism: The Road to Understanding and Evaluating It Through a Comparison With Realism
Ayşe Nur KANLI 171

Development of State Building Process and The Formation of a Political System in The Middle East
Kaan DİYARBAKIRLIOĞLU 181

STUDENT TEACHERS' PERCEPTIONS OF FORM-FOCUSED INSTRUCTION IN FOREIGN LANGUAGE CLASSES

Muhlise Coşgun ÖGEYİK[*]

Introduction

In recent decades, with intense theoretical and practical interests to grammar teaching, various recommendations have been put forward to contribute to language teaching field and to scaffold students to perceive and discover the features of the given language input. In foreign language education, it is known that a variety of occurrences may come about due to the nature of teaching procedures of teachers and expectations of students. Students' diverse personalities, styles, strategies, expectations, goals, and needs may also shape the framework of instructional manipulations. By taking such diverse issues into account, teachers can design language teaching policies and procedures through various approaches; in other words, the variety of grammar teaching approaches become inevitable due to diverse nature of teaching and learning environments. In this respect, the main principle for language education can be regulated to activate students' explicit and implicit knowledge. For doing this, form-focused instruction is suggested for language teaching (Ellis, 2006).

Focusing on form is expected to take students' attention to form either incidentally or in a planned way and thus language proficiency of students seems to be long-lasting (Long, 1991; Norris &

---

[*] Prof. Dr. Muhlise COŞGUN ÖGEYİK, Trakya University/TURKEY, ORCID: 0000-0002-0029-6409, muhlisecosgun@trakya.edu.tr.

Ortega, 2000; Ellis, 2006). It is also suggested that through form-focused instruction, students can acquire explicit knowledge of complex grammatical rules (Ellis, 2006). Additionally, students are encouraged to comprehend and use the elements of the target language from the start for communication (Larsen-Freeman, 2003) by noticing and discovering the workings of target language grammar (Schmidt, 2001). Three dimensions of grammar framework of any language have been explored by Larsen-Freeman (2003): form/structure; meaning/semantics; use/pragmatics. In this three dimensions, grammar teaching can be implemented either explicitly or implicitly or both in order to encourage student to discover the underlying rules of the target language. Discovery can be developed by students in a dynamic manner and contributes to the improvement of cognitive skills such as connecting, generalizing, and hypothesizing (Tomlinson, 1994). At any case of focusing on form either explicitly or implicitly, students' awareness levels are boosted towards the recognition of linguistic forms.

In recent years, in terms of form-focused instruction, a distinction has been made between Focus on Form (FoF) and Focus on Forms (FoFs). In FoF, grammar teaching is implemented in a planned or incidental way when necessary, while in FoFs grammar rules are introduced and practiced sequentially via controlled activities (Gass and Selinker, 2008). The purpose of using FoF and FoFs depends on students' needs and teachers' preferences in order to implement processing instruction in which students are expected to be active members as soon as they get the input and produce output.

In the literature, a variety of grammar teaching approaches have been suggested in order to address students' needs and expectations. The suggested approaches such as input enhancement, input enrichment, positive evidence, negative evidence, self-generated tasks, stimulated recall, and etc. are assumed to be prompting conscious registration of attended specific instances of language by processing formal features of the target language (Schmidt, 2010; Ortega, 2009; Swain, 2000).

In input enhancement the purpose is to take students' attention to the form within a context by highlighting the structure; the input is purposefully integrated into the instruction to teach the linguistic features of the target language. Input enrichment is manipulating the input to attract learners' attention to linguistic features; that is, enhancing the saliency of the structure through repeated usage. The attempt in *consciousness raising tasks* is to increase learners' ability to identify the given input consciously by noticing information for turning into knowledge (Mackey 2006). *Positive evidence* is based on forms that actually take place, while *negative evidence* deals with the information provided to a learner concerning the incorrectness of a form (Gass and Selinker, 2008). Another form of the input is to give students information about the target structure without giving students the full picture through only a partial explanation; that is *garden path*. In input processing, students may be exposed to *self-generated tasks* that can help students plan, monitor, and assess their own performance. At production stage, students can be encouraged to recall the given input and understand the ambiguities of the target language through *stimulated recall* or they can be directed to report and think about a task and activity after some interval via *task repetition* (Ellis 2003; Swain 2000).

Corrective feedback encourages learners to compare their own production with the feedback and to reformulate the incorrect linguistic form in various ways such as recasting, explicit correction, metalinguistic feedback, clarification questions, elicitation, repetition (Lightbown and Spada 2013; Bahrami 2010; Sadeghi and Heidaryan 2012; Rahi 2013): *recasts* are used during interaction without interrupting the communication through restating a learner's incorrect utterance for correcting implicitly; *explicit feedback* is to display the correct form to the learner explicitly by taking the attention of the learner to his or her own error; *metalinguistic feedback* is given by various comments, information, or questions relevant to the leaner's utterance in the direction of metalinguistic classification; the teacher asks *clarification requests* for making students notice the ill-formed utterance(s); to *elicit* the correct form, the teacher repeats the sentence of the student and pauses in the ill formed part and the student is expected to correct the incorrect form(s); and teachers *repeat* the ungrammatical utterance by using intonation to attract the learners' attention to the error. Students' attention to form can also be increased through *pushed output, self-generated or self-confronted* tasks in order to encourage students to plan, monitor, and assess their own performance (Ellis, 2003; Egi 2010).

Since language learning is both bottom-up and top-down processing, decoding specific information from the given input and produced output can be realized by means of explicit and implicit grammar teaching approaches for prompting discovery education and autonomous learning. Students' needs and expectations and teachers' decisions can shape the framework of grammar teaching. Therefore, this study was designed to reflect student teachers' perceptions of grammar teaching approaches.

Materials and Methods

In this study, interview sessions were arranged to investigate the student teachers' previous grammar learning experiences and their perceptions of grammar teaching approaches. For gathering data about their previous experiences, the student teachers were asked to fill a check list prepared to search for what approaches they had been exposed to while being instructed in grammar classes. To collect data about their perceptions of grammar teaching approaches, they were asked interview questions. The questions were delivered to the participants in written form, and they were asked to reflect their responses in written form as well. The collected data were analysed through content analysis.

Participants

The participants of the study were 28 student teachers of English attending a Turkish university. The data collected in a methodology course of the teacher training program.

Results

The data collected through checklist were analysed by means of percentage values. The results are displayed in Table 1.

Table 1. Student teachers' grammar learning experiences

I was taught through	Always %	Often %	Sometimes %	Never %
Explicit instruction	78	2	20	-
Implicit instruction	-	22	21	59
Input enhancement	-	10	12	78
Enriched input	-	8	10	88
Garden path	-	-	-	100
Positive evidence	36	46	18	-
Negative evidence	-	24	-	86
Stimulated recall	-	12	25	63
Self-generated tasks	-	18	22	60
Recasting	11	21	7	61
Elicitation	7	14	14	65
Explicit feedback	64	14	22	-
Metalinguistic feedback	86	14	-	-
Clarification requests	-	33	35	32

The student teachers' responses about their grammar learning experiences are listed in Table 1. As indicated in the table, the student teachers were exposed to explicit grammar teaching when they were students of English. Grammar instruction was carried out explicitly with mostly positive evidence; they were also treated explicitly through explicit feedback and metalinguistic feedback.

Table 2. Student teachers' perceptions and preferences of grammar teaching approaches

Categories of grammar teaching approaches	Mentions	%
Explicit instruction	10	4.2
Implicit instruction	27	10.5
Input enhancement	21	8.1
Enriched input	21	8.1
Garden path	8	4.0
Positive evidence	18	7.6
Negative evidence	7	3.9
Stimulated recall	16	7.4
Self-generated tasks	16	7.4
Recasting	6	3.8
Elicitation	8	4.0
Explicit feedback	32	11.3
Metalinguistic feedback	34	11.7
Clarification requests	20	8.0
TOTAL	244	100.00

As indicated in the table, the participants mostly were aware of implicit and explicit grammar teaching approaches. In their reflections, they mostly mentioned implicit grammar teaching in terms of input enhancement and input enrichment. For feedback category, they mostly mentioned metalinguistic feedback, explicit feedback, and clarification requests. This shows that the participants as prospective teachers preferred implicit teaching and giving the input implicitly. They, on the other hand, preferred to use explicit feedback for their students in the form of metalinguistic and clarification requests.

Discussion

In language learning, the preferences of teachers for teaching language skills and grammar are important. Therefore, this study investigated the background experiences of the student teachers of English and their perceptions of grammar teaching approaches in terms of their knowledge and their preferences. The results of the study for background experiences displayed that grammar teaching was employed as explicit teaching by focusing on the form; that is, by introducing and practicing grammar rules sequentially by means of controlled activities (Gass and Selinker, 2008). In input processing, they were exposed to mostly positive evidence. When they produced in the target language, mostly explicit and metalinguistic feedback were used to correct ungrammatical points. Thus, in formal education, they were exposed to traditional language teaching by not giving enhanced input or enriched input. In terms of tasks, they did not implement stimulated recall or self-generated tasks. At production level, recasting, elicitation, or clarification request were not used as feedback procedure. In the literature, it is suggested that by giving enhanced, enriched input types, by designing self-generated tasks or stimulated recalls, and by giving recasting, elicitation feedbacks, students may discover the grammar rules on their own and become more autonomous in learning process regarding the needs and expectations of the student (Schmidt, 2010; Lightbown and Spada 2013; Egi 2010).

The results of the research in terms of the student teachers' perceptions of grammar teaching were mostly based on implicit grammar teaching; that is, they preferred grammar teaching by giving enhanced input, enriched input in order to make students notice the given input and discover the rules on their own in a self-generated and autonomous way. However, for giving feedback, they preferred explicit feedback, metalinguistic explanations, and clarification requests. For giving feedback, various techniques such as recasting, explicit correction, metalinguistic feedback, clarification questions, elicitation, repetition, and etc. are suggested in the literature to prompt students' awareness levels about mismatches between their own production and given feedback in order to reformulate their production (Lightbown and Spada 2013; Sadeghi and Heidaryan 2012; Rahi 2013).

The responses of the student teachers confirm the gap between their language education process and their teacher training process. The similarity about their experiences and preferences was noticed in feedback types. They were exposed to explicit feedback and they agreed on giving explicit feedback as their preferences. In this respect, the brief answer to the question 'how should formal instruction take place in language teaching classes?' is that grammar teaching should be designed regarding the needs and expectations of the student. Grammar teaching should not be arranged in advance with a structural syllabus for all types of students. Grammar course content may be designed by taking the following suggestions into account:

- Putting communication first for its use in context should be the aim;
- Students should be reinforced in their communicative tasks;
- Students need to develop grammar knowledge as well as successful development of fluency and accuracy;
- Good performance of the student is shaped by how the student discovers and notices given rules.
- Grammar teaching should be designed regarding the needs and expectations of students;
- Grammar teaching can be designed by the control of the course teacher; for instance some teachers may have little control over the course content;

- Various factors such as diverse features of students, teacher cognition, the formal curriculum designed by schools, need to be taken into account while designing grammar courses.

Conclusion

In order to implement successful language teaching, teachers may tend to design their teaching practices by considering their personal thoughts about grammar teaching. It is admitted that in order to gain higher level of linguistic competence, focusing on form is a must. The type of the instruction for focusing on form may be either implemented by FoF or FoFs or both. The choice can be made for drawing students' attention to grammar implicitly or explicitly and teaching grammar should encompass language structure or sentence patterns, meaning and use. To conclude, Larsen-Freeman (2003:13) suggests that grammaring is the fifth skill: "When we view grammar as a skill, we are much more inclined to create learning situations that overcome the inert knowledge problem. We will not ask our students to merely memorize rules and then wonder why they do not apply them in communication".

References

Bahrami M 2010. The effect of task types on EFL learners' listening ability. URC Undergraduate Research Journal, 9. Retrieved July 2014 from: www.kon.org/urc/v9/bahrami.html

Egi T 2010. Uptake, modified output, and learner perceptions of recasts: Learner responses as language awareness. The Modern Language Journal, 94: 1–21.

Ellis R 2003. Task-based language learning and teaching. Cambridge: Cambridge University Press.

Ellis R 2006. Current issues in the teaching of grammar. TESOL Quarterly. 40(1):83-107.

Gass S M, Selinker L 2008. Second language Acquisition. New York: Routledge.

Larsen-Freeman D 2003. Teaching language: From grammar to grammaring. Boston, MA: Heinle and Heinle.

Lightbown P M, Spada N 2013. How languages are learned. Oxford: Oxford University Press.

Long M 1991. Focus on form: A design feature in language teaching methodology. In: Bot K, Ginsberg R, Kramsch C (Eds.), Foreign language research in cross-cultural perspective Amsterdam: John Benjamin, pp. 39-52.

Norris J, Ortega L 2000. Effectiveness of L2 instruction: A research synthesis and quantitative meta-analysis. Language Learning, 50: 417–528.

Mackey A 2006. Feedback, noticing and instructed second language learning. Applied Linguistics, 27: 405–430.

Ortega L 2009. Understanding second language acquisition. London: Hodder.

Rahi M 2013. The effect of explicit feedback on the use of language learning strategies: the role of instruction. Dil ve Edebiyat Eğitimi Dergisi, 2(5): 1-12.

Sadeghi B, Heidaryan H 2012. The effect of teaching pragmatic discourse markers on EFL learners' listening comprehension. English Linguistics Research, 1(2): 165-176.

Schmidt R 2001. Attention. In: P. Robinson (Ed.), Cognition and Second Language Instruction, Cambridge: Cambridge University Press, pp.3-32.

Schmidt R 2010. Attention, awareness, and individual differences in language learning. In: Chan W M, Chi S, Cin K N, Istanto J, Nagami M, Sew J W, Suthiwan, T, Walker I, Proceedings of CLaSIC, Singapore. December 2-4 pp. 721-737. Retrieved October, 2014 from: http://nflrc.hawaii.edu/PDFs/SCHMIDT

Swain M 2000. The output hypothesis and beyond: mediating acquisition through collaborative dialogue. In: Lantolf J P (Ed.). Sociocultural theory and second language learning. Oxford: Oxford University Press, pp.97-114.

Tomlinson B 1994. Pragmatic awareness activities. Language Awareness. 3(3): 119-129.

EMOTIONAL LOAD, FORMALITY, INFORMATIVENESS AND IMPLICATURE IN RELATION TO L2 WRITING PERFORMANCE

Kutay UZUN[*]

Introduction

In computer science and computational linguistics, NLP techniques have been widely used since 1960's, resulting in the advanced language processing and product development technologies that are in use today. Nonetheless, the use of NLP in language teaching/learning research has been somewhat limited in terms of the tools publicly available and a lack of studies regarding the NLP-based variables that bear potential to explain both comprehension and production. For this reason, NLP techniques, and the variables produced through them, should be studied in more detail with respect to language learning/teaching research for the purposes of explaining language comprehension and production along with developing new tools that can be used by learners, teachers and researchers.

The widely-used web-based NLP tools as of nowadays can be counted as the L2 Syntactic Complexity Analyzer (Lu, 2010), Web-based Lexical Complexity Analyzer (Ai & Lu, 2010), Coh-Metrix 3.0 (Graesser, McNamara, Louwerse & Cai, 2004) and Compleat Lexical Tutor (Cobb, 2021). With these pieces of software, researchers can quantify a number of syntactic complexity, lexical complexity, cohesion and discourse variables. Apart from the web-based soft-

---

[*] Trakya University, Faculty of Education, Department of English Language Teaching, ORCID Code: 0000-0002-8434-0832, kutayuzun@trakya.edu.tr.

ware, it is also possible to compute thousands of different indices regarding readability, n-grams, errors, sentiments, intertextual cohesion along with lexical and syntactic complexity by using free and downloadable NLP-based software presented by Kyle (2021) on www.kristopherkyle.com. Although all these tools combined can provide most of the data that may be needed in a language learning/teaching context, NLP as an ever-growing field demonstrates constant development that should be caught up with by researchers of language pedagogy, too.

One such opportunity presented by NLP specialists, that is yet to be explored within the context of language production, is emotion mining. Undoubtedly, emotions are a part of language production and in L2 writing, it has been shown that emotions such as satisfaction, surprise, happiness or negative emotions affect the way the act of writing is actualized (Mahfoodh, 2017). Moreover, sentiments as reflected in L2 texts seem to influence both syntactic complexity (Wang, 2020) and essay quality (Uzun & Ulum, in review). Given the relationship between emotions and written performance in L2, emotion mining stands out as a technique to explore the construct of L2 writing deeper.

In addition to emotion, academic writing in both L1 and L2 is required to demonstrate certain stylistic qualities. Formality is one of those qualities, requiring writers to follow certain formatting and stylistic conventions in academic texts (Bui, 2018). Hyland and Jiang (2017) articulate that formality increases the informativeness of academic texts by reducing the level of ambiguity. Similarly, Heylighten and Deweale (1999) state that a formal style is marked by a higher level of informativeness and explicitness in addition to impersonality and accuracy. Based on these findings and suggestions, it can be said that academic writing is conventionally formal, informative and explicit. Given these features, then, it is possible to argue that the computational analysis of those features in academic texts bears meaning for language learning/teaching research in addition to other branches of science.

The literature relevant to language learning/teaching indicates numerous NLP tools that can be used by language researchers.

However, the developments in NLP also bear implications for language learning/teaching, necessitating testing recent measurement methods within the learning/teaching context. In addition, it is understood from the literature that emotional load, formality, informativeness and implicature are relevant variables to L2 academic writing but the computational insights provided by NLP techniques regarding those variables are yet to be explored within the context of L2 writing. For this reason, this study aims to see if those variables can explain L2 academic writing performance with the following research questions:

1. Does emotional load predict undergraduate L2 academic writing performance?
2. Do formality, informativeness and implicature predict undergraduate L2 academic writing performance?

Materials and Methods

Since the study aimed to predict L2 academic writing performance through emotional load, formality, informativeness and implicature in quantifiable terms, a quantitative methodology was preferred.

The corpus of the study consisted of 185 literary analysis essays written by 185 students of English Language Teaching at a public university in Turkey. The same corpus was used in several other studies of the author such as Uzun (in review) and Uzun and Ulum (in review). The corpus consisted of a sum of 61871 word tokens and 4349 types. The averages were 334.44 tokens and 23.51 types for each essay. All the essays in the corpus were reliably scored between 0 and 100 by means of the Genre-Based Literary Analysis Essay Scoring Rubric (Uzun & Topkaya, 2020).

In addition to the scores already present in the corpus, emotional load, formality, informativeness and implicature data for each essay was generated using Python 3.8.5. Emotional load was computed using the NRCLex Python library (Bailey, 2019) which is based on the NRC Emotion Lexicon (Mohammad & Turney, 2013). Accordingly, values between 0 and 1 regarding positivity, negativity, anger, anticipation, disgust, fear, joy, sadness, surprise and trust were obtained from the corpus. To compute formality, informativeness and implicature values, the squinky 0.1.0 Python library (Meyers, B. S., 2017) based on the SQUINKY! Corpus (Lahiri, 2015) and Vincze's (2015) feature selection study was utilized. Squinky is an NLP-based library which can provide formality/informality, informativeness/ambiguity and implicativeness/verbosity values between 0 and 1. The compilation of all these values formed the data source of the study.

For data analysis, machine learning algorithms were used since they provide advantage over traditional regression, having no assumption about data distribution and providing a number of algorithms that can be tested for the same purpose. In this study, J48, RandomForest, RandomTrees, Ibk, KStar, LWL, Logistic Regression, Simple Logistic Regression, SMO and Naive Bayes algorithms were tested in 10 iterations per algorithm and 10-fold Cross-validation using Weka 3.8.5 (Eibe, Mark & Witten, 2016). L2 writing performance was divided into two (low – high) and three levels (low – mid – high) using cluster analysis. Since the original data was imbalanced, data sets balanced by means of Synthetic Minority Oversampling Technique were also tested. For comparison, baseline classification accuracy percentages were also computed with ZeroR algorithm. They are presented below in Table 1.

Table 1. Baseline Accuracy Percentages

Variable	Two Performance Levels	Three Performance Levels
Emotional Load	70.27	42.16
Formality, Informativeness, Implicature	70.32	42.16

Spearman correlation analyses were also run to investigate the relationships between L2 writing performance and other variables since they would provide useful information in the interpretation of the results.

Results

Initially, descriptive results were produced for two and three-level performance groups. The essay scores for each group can be seen below in Table 2.

Table 2. Essay Scores for Performance Groups

Group	N_{Two-Level}	M	SD	Min	Max
Two Levels					
Low	55	32.89	10.37	8	47
High	130	64.37	10.93	48	97
Three Levels					
Low	49	31.29	9.84	8	44
Mid	78	55.49	5.89	45	65
High	58	74.41	6.96	66	97

Following the essay scores, emotional loads were also computed for each performance cluster. The results for the two-level performance groups are presented in Table 3.

Table 3. Emotional Loads for Two Performance Groups

Group	Value	Fear	Anger	Trust	Surprise	Positive	Negative	Sadness	Disgust	Joy	Anticipation
Low	M	0.13	0.10	0.12	0.05	0.17	0.16	0.07	0.05	0.06	0.08
	SD	0.05	0.05	0.05	0.03	0.08	0.06	0.03	0.03	0.04	0.03
	Min	0.00	0.00	0.03	0.00	0.04	0.05	0.00	0.00	0.00	0.00
	Max	0.21	0.20	0.27	0.13	0.35	0.30	0.13	0.12	0.15	0.16
High	M	0.13	0.11	0.12	0.05	0.17	0.16	0.07	0.05	0.06	0.08
	SD	0.05	0.05	0.04	0.02	0.08	0.05	0.03	0.03	0.04	0.04
	Min	0.02	0.01	0.02	0.00	0.03	0.02	0.00	0.00	0.00	0.01
	Max	0.22	0.21	0.25	0.16	0.35	0.25	0.14	0.12	0.18	0.19

The emotional load results for the three-level performance groups can be seen in Table 4.

Table 4. Emotional Loads for Three Performance Groups

Group	Value	Fear	Anger	Trust	Surprise	Positive	Negative	Sadness	Disgust	Joy	Anticipation
Low	M	0.13	0.10	0.12	0.05	0.18	0.16	0.07	0.05	0.06	0.08
	SD	0.04	0.05	0.05	0.03	0.07	0.06	0.03	0.03	0.04	0.03
	Min	0.06	0.00	0.03	0.00	0.04	0.05	0.00	0.00	0.00	0.00
	Max	0.21	0.20	0.27	0.13	0.35	0.30	0.13	0.12	0.15	0.16
Mid	M	0.14	0.12	0.11	0.05	0.16	0.16	0.08	0.05	0.06	0.08
	SD	0.05	0.05	0.04	0.02	0.08	0.06	0.03	0.03	0.04	0.04
	Min	0.00	0.02	0.02	0.00	0.03	0.05	0.00	0.00	0.00	0.01
	Max	0.22	0.21	0.25	0.11	0.35	0.25	0.14	0.12	0.18	0.19
High	M	0.12	0.10	0.12	0.05	0.20	0.15	0.06	0.04	0.07	0.08
	SD	0.05	0.05	0.04	0.03	0.07	0.05	0.03	0.03	0.04	0.03
	Min	0.02	0.01	0.03	0.00	0.05	0.02	0.00	0.00	0.00	0.01
	Max	0.22	0.21	0.22	0.16	0.35	0.25	0.13	0.12	0.14	0.15

After the descriptive results, prediction algorithms were run on Weka. The results of the prediction analysis, showing how well emotional load could predict two-level imbalanced, two-level balanced, three-level imbalanced and three-level balanced data are tabulated below in Table 5.

Table 5. Emotional Load Prediction Accuracy Percentages

Algorithm	Two Levels, Imbalanced	Two Levels, Balanced	Three Levels, Imbalanced	Three Levels, Balanced
Ibk	57.62	57.62	34.82	39.81
KStar	59.27	59.27	31.90	31.90
LWL	68.91	68.91	35.11	35.11
NaiveBayes	65.64	65.64	**42.43**	**42.43**
Logistic	69.14	69.14	38.81	38.81
SMO	**70.32**	**70.32**	40.63	41.01
Simple Logistic	69.57	69.57	41.93	41.93
RandomTree	58.52	58.52	34.80	34.80
RandomForest	66.79	66.79	39.81	39.81
J48	69.45	69.45	34.11	34.11

Considering that the baseline accuracy levels were 70.27 for the two-level data set and 42.16 in the three-level data set, it was seen that the emotional load in the corpus could make a significant contribution to prediction accuracy in neither the balanced nor the imbalanced models. Indeed, correlation analyses showed that none of the emotional load variables were significantly correlated with essay scores ($p > .05$) except for positive emotions, which resulted in a correlation coefficient of .197 ($p < .01$) which could explain only 4% of the variance. In that respect, this significant correlation coefficient was also negligible and it probably resulted from a false discovery.

The descriptive results for formality, informativeness and verbosity divided by each performance cluster are presented below in Table 6.

Table 6. Formality, Informativeness and Verbosity Values

Group	Value	Formality	Informativeness	Verbosity
Two Groups				
Low	M	0.72	0.98	0.08
	SD	0.41	0.13	0.24
	Min	0.00	0.03	0.00
	Max	1.00	1.00	0.95
High	M	0.77	0.99	0.06
	SD	0.38	0.09	0.21
	Min	0.00	0.00	0.00
	Max	1.00	1.00	1.00
Three Groups				
Low	M	0.76	0.98	0.09
	SD	0.39	0.14	0.25
	Min	0.00	0.03	0.00
	Max	1.00	1.00	0.95
Mid	M	0.71	0.98	0.06
	SD	0.41	0.12	0.21
	Min	0.00	0.00	0.00
	Max	1.00	1.00	0.99
High	M	0.81	1.00	0.05
	SD	0.36	0.03	0.19
	Min	0.00	0.79	0.00
	Max	1.00	1.00	1.00

Following the descriptive results, prediction analyses were run for all groups, including the balanced data sets. The results can be seen below in Table 7.

Table 7. Formality, Informativeness and Verbosity Prediction Accuracy Percentages

Algorithm	Two Levels, Imbalanced	Two Levels, Balanced	Three Levels, Imbalanced	Three Levels, Balanced
Ibk	56.51	52.74	41.09	46.01
KStar	68.30	62.34	37.19	45.84
LWL	68.47	52.38	40.35	37.07
NaiveBayes	62.55	46.84	30.32	32.85
Logistic	69.40	49.39	40.25	36.47
SMO	69.73	49.12	40.54	36.31
Simple Logistic	70.10	47.34	41.73	35.91
RandomTree	70.05	62.90	**42.32**	47.62
RandomForest	**70.32**	**63.60**	41.95	**51.11**
J48	**70.32**	49.68	40.49	38.47

The baseline accuracy percentages in the formality, informativeness and verbosity model were 70.32 for the two-level data set and 42.16% for the three-level data set. Based on these findings, both the balanced and the imbalanced models could not predict L2 writing performance successfully. The lack of a relationship between those values and essay scores was also confirmed by correlation analysis, none of which yielded statistically significant results ($p > .05$).

Discussion

The results indicated that computationally-obtained emotional load values for fear, anger, trust, surprise, positivity, negativity, sadness, disgust, joy and anticipation could not predict L2 academic writing performance at a practically useful level. Moreover, those values were not significantly related to literary analysis essay scores. Even though the emotional state of a language learner influences his/her performance in L2 writing (Mahfoodh, 2017), the findings of this study did not bear the same results. This suggests that the emotional load present in a text and the emotional state of a learner are essentially different constructs although the text might be influenced by the learner's emotional state.

It was also seen in the result that formality, informativeness and verbosity values could not successfully predict L2 academic writing performance. Similar to emotional load values, the relationships between essay score and each of those values were not significantly related to literary analysis essay score. These results contradict those of Bui (2018), Hyland and Jiang (2017) and Heylighten and Deweale (1999). However, I believe questioning the efficiency of the measurement is a better option to explain this contradiction since common sense dictates that academic texts in any language should be formal, informative and verbose. On the other hand, the measurement of those concepts in this study are based on a sentence-based logistic regression model lacking 100% accuracy. In that respect, the lack of a relationship between formality, informativeness and verbosity should not be attributed to the absence of an actual relationship, but to the possible insufficiency of the measurement technique.

Conclusion

The study showed that textually-present emotional load, measured as fear, anger, trust, surprise, positivity, negativity, sadness, disgust, joy and anticipation could not predict L2 academic writing performance. Interestingly, computationally-obtained formality, informativeness and verbosity could not predict performance, either. These findings indicate that the emotional load in a text and the emotional state of a language learner are actually different constructs that should be measured using different methods. Moreover, considering that formality, informativeness and verbosity are universal requirements in academic writing, the available method to measure those constructs computationally does not seem to be sufficient for L2 academic writing research.

Although the experiment itself failed in this study, practically useful implications can still be drawn. Firstly, the findings of the study, contradicting those of other emotion studies in L2 contexts, signify the difference between textual emotional load and a learner's emotional state. However, how emotional state might be interacting with textual emotional load is still to be researched. Moreover, the findings show that the current methods in the computational measurement for formality, informativeness and verbosity, which are all crucial, cannot explain performance in L2 academic writing. Therefore, the findings call for more powerful methods, preferably utilizing textual features such as complexity and part-of-speech, for the measurement of those constructs in L2 contexts for practically-useful applications.

References

Ai H, Lu X 2013. A corpus-based comparison of syntactic complexity in NNS and NS university students' writing. In Ana Díaz-Negrillo, Nicolas Ballier, and Paul Thompson (eds.), Automatic Treatment and Analysis of Learner Corpus Data. Amsterdam/Philadelphia: John Benjamins, pp. 249-264

Bailey MM 2019. NRCLex [Software]. Retrieved from https://pypi.org/project/NRCLex/

Bui G 2018. A lexical approach to teaching formality in freshman L2 academic writing. In LT Wong, WLH Wong, Teaching and learning English for academic purposes: Current research and practices. New York, NY: Nova Science Publishers, pp. 111-124.

Cobb T 2021. The compleat lexical tutor [Software]. Retrieved from http://www.lextutor.ca

Eibe F, Hall MA, Witten IH 2016. The WEKA Workbench. Online Appendix for "Data Mining: Practical Machine Learning Tools and Techniques" (4th ed.), Morgan Kaufmann. Retrieved from https://www.cs.waikato.ac.nz/ml/weka/Witten_et_al_2016_appendix.pdf

Graesser AC, McNamara DS, Louwerse MM, Cai Z 2004. Coh-metrix: analysis of text on cohesion and language. Behav Res Methods Instrum Comput. 36(2):193-202. doi: 10.3758/bf03195564.

Heylighen F, Dewaele JM 1999. Formality of language: definition, measurement and behavioral determinants [Technical Report]. Interner Bericht, Center "Leo Apostel", Vrije Universiteit Brüssel, 4.

Hyland K, Jiang FK 2017. Is academic writing becoming more informal? English for Specific Purposes, 45: 40-51.

Kyle K 2021. Kristopher Kyle – Tools. Retrieved from http://www.kristopherkyle.com/tools.html

Lahiri S 2015. SQUINKY! A corpus of sentence-level formality, informativeness, and implicature. Ann Arbor, 1001, 48109. Retrieved from https://arxiv.org/pdf/1506.02306.pdf

Lu X 2010. Automatic analysis of syntactic complexity in second language writing. International Journal of Corpus Linguistics, 15(4):474-496.

Mahfoodh OHA 2017. "I feel disappointed": EFL university students' emotional responses towards teacher written feedback. Assessing Writing, 31: 53-72.

Meyers BS 2017. Squinky 0.1.0 [Software]. Available at https://pypi.org/project/squinky/

Mohammad SM, Turney PD 2013. NRC emotion lexicon [Technical Report]. National Research Council, Canada, 2.

Uzun K "in review". Using rhetorical writing frames to enhance negotiated independent construction in L2 writing.

Uzun K, Ulum ÖG "in review". Sentiment and sentence similarity as predictors of L2 writing performance.

Vincze V 2015. Uncertainty detection in natural language texts (Unpublished PhD Thesis). University of Szeged, Hungary.

Wang Y 2020. Emotion and syntactic complexity in L2 writing: A corpus-based study on Chinese college-level students' English writing. The Asian Journal of Applied Linguistics, 7(1): 1-17.

METROPOLITAN URBAN MANAGEMENT AND EFFECTS OF COVID-19 PANDEMIC ON METROPOLITAN CITY MANAGEMENT IN ITALY

*Melike KAYIRAL**
*Mesut KAYAER***

Introduction

In the last quarter of the 20th century, sustainability and sustainable urban development have come to the forefront in order to solve urban problems, re-establish the relationship between development and the environment. Increasing the ecological, ecenomic, political and social problems faced by cities and exceeding the city limits, inclusion of a large number of actors and with the technological developments have been formed complex urban structures increasingly. After the industrial revolution with growing cities rapidly began a massive migration from rural areas towards the cities. Accelerated urbanization and intensive migration led to the emergence of a metropolitan urban understanding. As a result of such rapid growth the number of megacities has increased day by day. These areas are the most obvious indicator of today's urbanization processes. Managing all aspects of these areas depends on the existence of strong corporate structures. Within this framework, it is possible to take institutionalization efforts to metropolitan city governments in Italy until the 1990s. In this respect, the

---
* Bartın University Graduate School of Political Science and Public Administration Doctoral Program, Turkey, Orcid: 0000-0003-2147-0928, meliksahleyla5880@gmail.com.
** Dr., Bartın University Political Science and Public Administration, Turkey, Orcid: 0000-0002-3682-5958, mkayaer@bartin.edu.tr.

date of 2001 is important for the constitutional status of metropolitan city governments as a unit of local government. For regions that have gained metropolitan city ctatus, a new administrative organization has been established outside the traditional structure at the level of local governments. Local governments which are the administrative units closest to the source of the problem in terms of meeting the common needs in local and playing a fundamental role in providing effective and efficient public services are both part of the changing development approach and the center of development policies. This position of local authorities places important responsibilities on these units in terms of their duties. In order to successfully manage the process in the face of social, ecenomic and political crises faced by nations, central government and local government collabration skills are critical. Ensuring public confidence in the political decisions taken at this point is a key element of social peace and health. Prerequisites for success in fighting the Covid-19 pandemic, which has affected the world; require policies determined under the guidance of reason and science, in addition to health institutions, the spirit of struggle and collective solidarity on a community basis. In this context, it is an important strategy for the government to be in a direction in the fight against the epidemic, which leaves its local administrations autonomous, convinces the whole of society and engages in the fight. Another important pillar of the strategy is that it can subsidize its citizens in this process. From the perspective of Italy, related to the situation in question the heads of regional governments publish regulations in addition to the national regulation or seems to aggravate the conditions according to the critical rating of the outbreak. As part of the study, created to reseacrh the literature and quoting the necessary statistical information from official source, information will be provided related to the metropolitan city management system of Italy. General situation of the Covid-19 pandemic and its impact on metropolitan city administrations will be examined from the perspective of the cooperation ability of central government and local authorities.

Local Government in Italy

The relationship between the cenral administration and the local administrations, which constitute the two basic levels of the public administration system in a country is very important. Local governments are autonomous institutions serving in order to be better central government, exist local democracy, respond more quickly and effectively to the needs and demands of the people. The fact that local administrations have a strong position against the central administration also determines the limits of the autonomy of these administrations. In the ability of these administrations to be autonomous; in order to ensure the integrity of the administration, local authorities are supervised by the central government a clear definition of the boundaries of administrative custody control is important for maintaining autonomy. This relationship between central and local varies from contry to country. Therefore, the scope of the relationship between central administration and local administrations, the powers and duties of local governments are different from each other (Eryılmaz, 2009: 80-88).

In Italy, important struggles have finally taken place to achieve the legal status of local and regional governments. Italy, which has gone through various stages in its history, as of June 30, 2004, has an administrative structure with a total of 20 autonomous regions within the unitary management structure impending 5 in special status and 15 in ordinary status. In the fifth section of the Italian constitution of 1948, local governments are counted as regions, provinces and municipalities. In the country, it is not possible for provinces and municipalities to act independently of state and regional policies. Municipalities and provinces have gained a stronger position, in 1982 with the law on local administrations enacted. Italy has significantly expanded the autonomy of local governments, in 1990, 2001 and 2003, through local government reforms. Thus, for the autonomy of local governments the public authority has been revised with an understanding from local to central. Local governments have become closer to the public and municipalities which are the smallest unit of local governments have been brought to the fore (Marchetti, 2010: 91; Ulusoy ve Akdemir, 2006: 127).

The Italian constitution defines the state as one and indivisible and recognizes local autonomy: "The Republic is divided into regions, provinces and communes. Communes, provinces, metropolitan cities and regions are autonomous organizations with unique statutes, powers and responsibilities according to the principles set out in the law"

(1948 Italian Constitution, a. 114). The Constitution ranks local governments as regions, provinces and communes. Accordingly, this structure, which corresponds to its unitary structure and protects the uniqueness and indivisibility of the state, is autonomous within its authority and status. Special status units have more legislative and executive powers than ordinary regions. The most important reason for making such a distinction in regional administration is to prevent intransigence. Another pillar of the country's local government units are the provinces. Provincial administrations with a total number of 103 can perform functions in a limited capacity. Within the scope of local government units, the closest administrative units to the public are minicipalities (Ulusoy ve Akdemir, 2006:127-128).

District Administration

Regional administrations, which are an administrative unit above local administrations, have more far-reaching powers than provinces and municipalities. In addition to the administrative powers of these administrative units, they also have legislative powers. The bodies of these administrations, which are defines as autonomous geographical units, come to work by election. Organizational structures and functions of regional governments vary regionally (Ulusoy ve Akdemir, 2013: 152). There are 20 regional administrations in the country, fifteen ordinary anf five special status. Section 118 of the 1948 Constitution duties of these administrations according to the article; sortable such as the provision of health and social welfare services, agriculture and forestry, regional transport and urban services, local museum and library services, the tourism and hospitality industry services, urban and rural police services, fire brigade, locations and marketplace services, other tasks can be listed as given by laws (1948 Italian Constitution).

Provinces

The location of the provinces in Italy is in the form of two separate administrative structures, the provincial unit of the central administration and the local administrative unit. Although provinces have a larger area than municipalities as a geographical area since the establishment of the country, they have not been as effective as municipalities. Functions of provincial administrations, which constitute the weakest link among local administrative units; limited to a few specific areas such as protection of public order, construction and repair of roads, determination of tax and fee rates, determination and management of budget, support of secondary schools and high schools, environmental protection and social services. Provincial administrations in this context; tasks are undertaken such as conservation of water and energy resources, disaster management, environment and the protection of cultural assets, the garbage management system implementation at the provincial level, water flow regulation, hygiene, and preventive health care tasks, arts and vocational education, technical and administrative assistance to local governments, in cooperation with municipalities, economic, commercial, social, cultural, tourist and sporting activities in the sectors coordinate and promote (1948 Italian Constitution).

The union of the provincial administration are the Provincial Council, the Provincial Council and the Provincial President. The number of members of the council, which is the decision making union, varies between 24-45 according to the population of the province. Assembly elected for 4 years elects a president from within its own institution. Representation in parliament is carried out on the basis of the relative representation system and according to the parties that hold the majority. The party that gets most of the vote gets 60 percent of the seats, the rest are distributed proportionally among other lists (Ulusoy ve Akdemir, 2013: 154). The provincial assembly gives its opinion to the governor (Baccetta, 2013: 24; Karabaş, 1991: 62). The provincial council is the executive unity. The number of members does not exceed one-fifth of the number of members of Parliament. The Council is responsible for the execution of all administrative works not granted by law to the provincial council, the provincial president or the central administration. The council is responsible for implementing the decisions of the assembly and has the power to bring proposals to the assembly. The provincial president, elected popularly is the other unit of provincial government. The council may decide on the appointment of its members and withdraw from membership if necessary. The provincial president, responsible for appointing government representatives in affiliated administrations. The president is responsible for ensuring and supervising the performance of duties within the framework of the legislation (Küçük, 2019: 17).

Municipalities

Municipalities in Italy, fulfill not included in the mandate of the state and other local units such as economic development, administrative duties on social services, space use and regulation, military service, statistics, population records and electoral services, municipal duties within the framework of the law. These duties are assigned to the mayor in the capacity of representing the state. It is also possible to grant other duties to municipalities by law. However, in such a case, it is necessary to transfer sufficient financial resources to perform these tasks. In Italy, municipalities play a central role in national life and reflect an entrenched feature of the political system. Municipalities with more than 8000 numbers have three units: municipal council, municipal committee and mayor (Geray, 1997: 55; Ulusoy & Akdemir, 2006:130).

The Municipal Council that is decision-making unity of the municipality elected by the people for four year term. Although the upper and lower limits are not defined, the number of members is 12 in municipalities with a population of less than 3000, the number of members is 60 people in places with more than 5000. The

Council, the executive body of the municipality consist of the mayor and members designated by dual numbers (Ulusoy ve Akdemir, 2013: 155). The mayor elected by the people is the other unit of the municipality. Mayor represents the municipality and is the head of the Municipal Council and Municipal Administration. Therefore, the implementation of the decisions taken, the management of the municipality and the supervision of the works are under the authority of the mayor (Tortop, 1996: 67).

Audit of Local Governments

Because of Italy has a unitary administrative system, a heavy administrative guardianship is exercised over local administrations. According to the article 125. of the Constitution, " Custody control over the operations of the region is carried out by state units within the procedures and principles established by the laws of the Republic; for this purpose, it says that administrative judicial bodies are created". In accordance with this article of the Constitution, the operations and actions of local administrations are mainly controlled by the central administration from the point of view of compliance with the constitution and other laws or controlled through commissions created on its behalf (1948 Italian Constitution).

Decisions of the executive branch are overseen at the request of the Executive Council of the local government council or some of the councillors. Decisions are considered effective if they are not canceled by the committee within 20 days. If the municipal or provincial council commits unconstitutional acts, seriously violates the law, commits a serious public order crime, does not elect executive rules or political responsible within 60 days, they will be terminated by Presidential Decree (Ulusoy & Akdemir, 2006:134).

Following the Italian constitution of 1948, which recognized and local allegiance, autonomy of regions, provinces and municipalities from political authority, also supported by the elections of 1970 is of great importance, especially in administrative tasks. They also provide partial financial autonomy through funding from official source.

Administrative Guardianship Over District Administration

The supervision of the laws of the region, which are prepared in accordance with the Constitution, is carried out by the governor of the region. District laws come into force after approval by the district administration. The governer has the authority to return it to the Regional Council for readjudication within 30 days if the laws of the region exceed the authority of the region and are contrary to national or regional utility (Olivetti, 2014: 148).

Control of the Actions And Operations of the District Administration

Audit of compliance with the laws of the actions and operations of the regional administration is maintained by the commission of audit. The commission is composed of judges, civil servants and experts, chaired by the regional governor. Decisions of the Regional Council, which are not canceled within 20 days, put into force. In case of violation of the laws, the units of the district administration shall be terminated. The termination process is carried out by decree of the Italian Presidency, after consultation with the parliamentary commission. In case of termination, three people from the public are appointed to the commission, who are qualified to be elected as members of Parliament, to be responsible for the administration until the new elections to be held within three month (Bilgiç, 1998: 561).

Administrative Guardianship Over Local Governments

Control over administrative actions and operations of provinces and municipalities is carried out by the regional audit committee. This commission consists of judges, law professors, civil servants like experts and members elected by the regional assembly. This audit is a legal audit, but decisions taken by Parliament are controlled. Decisions of the executive board are supervised at the request of the local government council, the board of directors or some of the councillors. Decisions put into force, if they are not cancelled by the committee within 20 day (Ulusoy ve Akdemir, 2001: 156-166).

Italy Metropolitan City Administration

According to the article 114. of the Constitution, metropolitan cities are also located between regions and provinces as local administrations. The local government reform, which was constitutionalized in 1990, envisioned the establishment of a metropolitan city system in large urban settlements, rather than the establishment of provincial local governments (1948 Italian Constitution). Metropolitan cities were included in the law as a local administrative unit together with the legal regulation in 2001 (Olivetti, 2014: 148). Metropolitan cities, like other local administrative units, have independent financial resources with income and expenditure autonomy (1948 Italian Constitution). The decision-making unit in metropolitan cities is the Metropolitan City Council. The formation of the Metropolitan City Council and the application of the rules for its election were adopted in the same way. The executive is the Metropolitan Giunta, similar to the provincial local administrations (Tortop, 1996: 66).

At the head of the Metropolitan administrations is the mayor of the Metropolitan. The president represents the Metropolitan Administration, makes appointments and heads the Giunta Council. The division of authority between the units of the Metropolitan Administration level is carried out in accordance with the general principles provided for the provincial local administration and municipalities. The Metropolitan Assembly makes basic decisions, directs and supervises its administrative units. Metropolitan mayor, represents the administration. The internal structure of the Metropolitan Administration is determined by the regulation of the organization and accepted by the Metropolitan City Council. According to the decisions taken by the state, the provisions on the status of employees are accepted with the collective labor agreement (Tortop, 1996: 66).

"The duties of metropolitan cities are roads, traffic, transport, planning, environmental protection, water and electricity services, economic development, health services in wider areas, vocational education, school services and urban services. Morever, metropolitan administrations have the authority to determine taxes and fees in relation to the services they perform" (Koçak, 2013: 408-409).

Covid-19 Pandemic in Italy

The Covid-19 pandemic, which originated in Wuhan, Hubei province, China and affected the entire world, continues to intensively engage the agenda in all countries. As of 06.05.2021, 155,888,185 cases have been identified worldwide, 133,350,966 people have healed and 3,257,615 have died (https://www.worldometers.info, Access: 07.05.2021). Therefore, there are currently 18,519,269 active cases. As of 07.05.2021, the number of doses of the vaccine was 1,170,942,729 (https://covid19.who.int/, Access: 07.05.2021). Looking at covid-19 data in Italy, 4,092,747 cases were identified, 3,572,713 people healed and 122,470 people died due to covid-19. The number of active cases is 397,564 (https://www.worldometers.info, Access: 07.05.2021). 22.64 million doses of the vaccine were inoculated (Ourworldindata.org, https://covid19.who.int/, Access: 07.05.2021). These numerical data also show that the covid-19 pandemic was the most dangerous pandemic in the modern era in terms of its effects on health, economy and social life.

The threat and danger posed by this virus, which cannot continue to exist outside the human body for a long time, should not be underestimated. Because the effect of this antigen, which causes a lot of complications and permanent damage on morbidity and mortality rates is also understood from numerical data. The emergence of new variants that mutate in different parts of the world, both increases the number of cases and causes various difficulties in terms of treatment studies.

In terms of the social, economic and political effects of restricted life defined as the new normal, in order not to be dragged into a global depression, obscurity and unpredictability, this process needs to be managed correctly all over the world. In this minval, resetting the number of cases and returning to normal life before the pandemic depends on a successful management process and the existence of social solidarity.

This pandemic has profoundly affected all countries, including developed countries. So that, developed Western countries have experienced serious crises because they have failed to prevent the spread of the disease and reduce death rates, or even managed the process unsuccessfully. Therefore, it has affected societies, countries and international systems in various ways, without distinction of developed or developing countries. Countries that are relatively successful are also shown as examples of other countries. Although differences in pandemic management and policies, social consciousness and sensitivities have stood out in these countries, the time and spees of taken decisions made directly affected the control of the pandemic. In this context, each country has been able to implement intervention in the process at different levels within the framework of its socio-economic and political forces. Within the scope of these measures, precaution have entered our lives such as informing the public, curfew restrictions, closing of workplaces, banning activities in public places, national and international travel restrictions, test policies, filiation methods.

The following table discusses the current situation of the pandemic in Italy and interventions for pandemic management.

Table 1. Covid-19 current data and Government Policies in Italy

Total Cases	4.092.747 (07.05.2021)
Total Deaths	122.470 (07.05.2021)
Toplam Testing	60.532.582 (07.05.2021)
Toplam Vaccine Dose	It was applied to 22.64 million people. (07.05.2021)
Number Of Active Cases in the Hospital	397.564 (07.05.2021)
Number of Casesin the Intensive Care Unit	2.253 (07.05.2021)
Number of Tests Per Confirmed Case In 1 Million	1.002.419 (07.05.2021)
Total Deaths Per 1 Million	2.022 (07.05.2021)
Death Rate Per Case (%)	2,992 (07.05.2021)
Total Number Of Patient Healed	3.572.713 (07.05.2021)
Vaccination Policy	All Vulnarable Groups
Testing Policy	Everyone with Symptoms

Information Campaigns	Coordinated Information Campaign, +2 meets the absolute Change determined by 2.00. (30.04.2021)
Income Support	Covers <50% of lost salary. (30.04.2021)
Debt and Contract Relief in Epidemic Period	Broad Relief (30.04.2021)
International Travel Restrict	Prohibited in high-risk areas. Some regional governments may also enforce this ban.
Contact Tracking	Comprehensive monitoring (all cases are monitored) (30.4.2021)
Cancellation of Public Events	Required Cancellations (30.04.2021)
Change Rate of Visitors to Public Event Areas Compared to the Pre-Pandemic Period	%6.86 (03.05.2021)
Workplace Closures	It is necessary for all, but other than key sector employees (pharmacy, food, etc.). (30.04.2021)
Public Transport Closures	Proposed closure (this restriction has been applied in some subnational areas) (30.04.2021)
Internal Motion Restrictions	Movements are restricted. It does not apply at all local levels, it has been applied in some sub-national regions. (30.04.2021)
Public Meeting Restrictions	<10 person (30.04.2021)
Closure of Schools	Required. (only on some levels) (30.04.2021)

Source: https://www.ecdc.europa.eu/en/publications-data/download-data-hospital-and-icu-admission-rates-and-current-occupancy-covid-19, https://www.worldometers.info/coronavirus/#countries, https://ourworldindata.org/grapher/public-transport-covid?region=Europe, https://covid19.who.int/, https://ourworldindata.org/covid-vaccinations?country=ITA, John Hopkins University Covid-19, Compiled from data.

The data in the table was created in accordance with the management and policies implemented in Italy. The country's success in managing the pandemic process is not effectively observed. One of the main parameters in the fight against the covid-19 pandemic is the tests. Countries that control the pandemic are expected to conduct fewer tests than countries where the outbreak has spread more widely. Therefore, this explains that the relationship between cases and tests is moving in the opposite direction, and the transmission is spreading rapidly. As of 07.05.2021, a total of 60,532,582 tests were conducted in Italy and 4,092,747 cases were detected. These numerical data show that Italy has not been able to fully manage the pandemic process successfully. Data in some countries in the European region are formed, such as Denmark 257.505 case, 41.474.152 test, Bulgaria 408.372 case, test 2.562.234, Austria 628.817 case, test 33.990.188, Finland 88.332 case, 4.165.178 test, Estonia 124.529 case, 1.318.022 test, Slovenia 245.159 case, test 1.199.033, Belgium 1.007.264 case, test 12.821.364, Germany 3.497.527 case, test 56.836.969, Spain 3.581.392 case, test 47.213.067.

These numerical data show that Italy is partly less successful than some countries in the European region. However, when evaluated within the framework of the latest data, it can be said that it is in better condition than France with the number of 5,728,090 cases and 77,792,623 tests (https://www.worldometers.info/coronavirus/#countries, Access: 07.05.2021).

Italy can be explained by reasons such as passive management in the pandemic process, especially at the initial stage, slower movement in the detection of initial cases, policies and strategies carried out, the country's management system, the current political and economic situation. The excess of the elderly population and the inadequate capacity of the health system in the face of this situation led to the rapid transformation of the process into a health crisis. In this context, it may be mentioned about the relationship and cooperation between the central government and regional governments, which is the subject of the study, is reflected in the current situation at the point of controlling and managing the pandemic process. Although there are different forms of management and different legal processes, regional governments in high-risk metropolitan cities of the country, can impose travel restrictions, adopt additional regulations and implement additional measures, unlike the national decree.

Covid-19 Pandemic Challenge of Central Government and Local Governments in Italy

Cities are the determining factor of social health management in a country. In today's world, city management increases the importance of local administrations. The local authorities responsible for managing the city also carry out many services related to the health of the community. The scope of these services ranges from environmental services to epidemic prevention to qualifications that reduce the impact of socio-economic problems in the city. Therefore, epidemic periods require joint work of local institutions and organizations in a city. The responsibilities assumed by local governments brought social municipality to the forefront, and the importance of the principle of subsidiarity was felt more in this process. As part of the measures taken against the pandemic in Italy, the decree of the prime minister was put into effect on 06.11.2020. In the national decree, areas where the pandemic is high are classified as risk areas. In this classification, the riskiest area is classified as red, the medium-risk area is classified as orange, and the low-risk area is classified as yellow (https://www.governo.it/it/articolo/domande-frequenti-sulle-misure-adottate-dal-governo, Access: 04.05.2021).

Less risky yellow areas; citizens can go out after 22:00 by presenting their health, work and essential status with a declaration. Maximum capacity in regional rail and local transport was limited to 50%, and private sector and public employment exams were postponed. Citizens have been advised not to travel by private car and public transport during the day, except for reasons such as education, health and work.

Medium-risk orange areas; in addition to the measures applied in low-risk areas, in the declaration submitted, travel within and outside the region is prohibited except for emergency and medical needs.

High-risk red areas; in addition to the measures in other regions, outdoor sports activities have been decimated, and cafeterias, restaurants and bakeries have been closed (https://ticaret.gov.tr/yurtdisi-teskilati/avrupa/italya/ulke-profili/kovid-19-gelismeleri, Access: 05.05.2021).

The national decree of 24.10.2020 applies to all of Italy. In addition, the Lombardy regional administration has issued an additional regulation to prevent the spread of the epidemic due to high risk. Conditions are aggravated by the regulation. Accordingly, 623 decree on 21.10.2020 was issued exclusively for the regions of Lombardy and Milan. In the contents of 623 Decree; subject to restrictions such as restrictions on night out, Prohibition of alcohol consumption in public places, distance education, etc. (https://www.esteri.it/mae/en/ministero/normativaonline/decreto-iorestoacasa-domande-frequenti/focus-cittadini-italiani-in-rientro-dallestero-e-cittadini-stranieri-in-italia.html, Access: 04.05.2021).

The Council of ministers declared the OHAL for the first time nationally on January 31, 2020 with a period of 6 months, after that, extended from January October 15, 2020 to January 31, 2021. A new cabinet decree was issued on October 13, 2020 with a one-month term, this decree partially amended the regulations on domestic and international travel. In addition, travel restrictions have been imposed on certain regions, some restrictions have been placed on those coming from foreign regions and certain states (https://www.gazzettaufficiale.it/eli/id/2020/10/13/20A05563/sg, Access: 04.05.2021). In this context, regional governments have required certain rules to be followed by certain regions and certain designated foreign countries. It is remarked that additional provisions on the restriction imposed in different parts of the country for those who go to Italy, by contacting the regional authorities directly or they must obtain it by checking the relevant web pages (http://www.regioni.it/regioni-online/, https://www.gazzettaufficiale.it/dettaglioArea/12, Access: 04.05.2021).

Regional government of Lombardy; 275 Decree was approved by the Cabinet on the proposal of Prime Minister Mario Draghi and Health Minister Roberto Speranza. By this decree, it is stipulated that the OHAL will be extended until July 31, 2021, depending on the state of emergency health (https://www.regione.lombardia.it/wps/portal/istituzionale/HP/coronavirus/misure, Access: 04.05.2020).

Ordinances of the Presidency Of The Region Of Campania; As part of measures related to the Covid-19 pandemic, by the regional presidency, 96., 97., 98. and 99. numbered regulations (10.12.2020-20.12.2020) and 1., 2., 3., 14., 15., 16. and 17. numbered regulations (05.01.2021- 06.05 2021) have been published. Regulations in question, in accordance with the national decree, it is organized to impose some restrictions and make changes in according to the potential risk situation of the region (http://www.regione.campania.it/regione/it/la-tua-campania/coronavirus-kyxz/ordinanze-del-presidente-della-regione-campania, https://www.governo.it/it/articolo/domande-frequenti-sulle-misure-adottate-dal-governo/15638#zone, Access: 04.05.2021).

Regulation 96: Following the emergence of Covid-19 health risks and the emergence of diseases caused by infectious viral agents, OHAL was extended until October 15, 2020 in the national territory. This regulation was adopted in order to control the health risks arising from the spread of the Covid-19 virus and counteract the risks that are likely to arise.

Regulation 97: In order to ensure the safe conduct of activities, it was emphasized that health monitoring data should be transmitted daily to the Higher Institute of the Ministry of Health by the regions.

Regulation 98: Regions were allowed to introduce restrictive and relaxing measures on condition that they inform the Ministry of Health.

Regulation 99: In this context, some decisions have been taken such as avoiding the risks of spreading the new variant of the virus, the effects of the virus still persist, 14 days isolation process for the risks associated with the arrival of citizens on the territory of the region and about conducting the necessary checks.

Regulation 1: Due to the high increase in the number of cases, it was decided to move to a special and very sensitive management stage on a national and regional scale. Emergency measures have been taken in connection with the launch of the vaccination campaign.

Regulation 2: Taking into account the importance of education and training, decisions have been taken to initiate face to face training according to the regional risk height.

Regulation 3: In this context, In the Naples and Campania regions, the start of face to face training for secondary schools was suspended and regional heads remain in contact with monitoring boards according to the number of cases, and it was decided to start training activities according to the risk situation.

Regulation 14: It was decided to start training in low risk yellow and orange areas. It has been decided that the regional heads will remain in contact with the health departments and take measures to prevent the high spread of the Covid-19 virus or its variants in schools and that decommissioning again if necessary.

Regulation 15: As part of the monitoring of regional crisis units, it was decided to start commercial activities according to the decrease in the percentage of positive cases and the decrease in the number of cases.

Regulation 16: It was issued to initiate vaccination studies in the Campania region.

Regulation 17: It was decided that regional crisis units should be authorized. It is envisaged that certain measures and rules can be introduced in accordance with the current case and the course of the pandemic, ensuring the promotion of e-safe reception and use and in this context, it was decided to initiate the necessary interventions. Services in various areas such as tourism, hotels, weddings, transportation, etc. have been made possible by providing security.

Conclusion

The conclusion of the study is that it is possible to mention the existence of coordination between the central government and local administrations in Italy. It seems that the central government is trying to manage the pandemic process without interfering with the autonomy of local governments. This situation is also understood from the regulations made in the legislation. Although the pandemic has been controlled by vaccination studies, high cases and deaths have been observed, especially due to strategies implemented at the beginning of the process. Therefore, it is not possible to say that the process has achieved success in its management with 4,092,747 cases and 122,470 deaths. It is also seen that the perception of social risk is not fully formed . Because the change in the frequency of use of public spaces compared to the period before the pandemic is 6.86 %, and the high number of visitors to the public space in times without restrictions indicates this situation. It may be possible to close this vacancy through educational programs organized by local institutions. On the other hand, it can be said that the economic support provided by the public in line with the economic power of the state also has a relatively positive effect.

It is possible to say that metropolitan city administrations have been able to work actively in the pandemic process relatively, have taken various initiatives in order to overcome financial difficulties and have been able to make independent decisions about the pandemic. So that, mayor of Milan Giuseppe Sala established the Mutual Aid Fund, collecting aid from individual donors and the private sector, this fund, also approved by the City Council, € 3 million has been added to the allowance for emergency assistance. The fund was established to support citizens affected by the economic downturn due to the shutdown, commercial organizations, associations, unemployed, discontinuous workers, temporary workers whose contracts were not renewed due to the closure in the pandemic process. In addition, the municipality of Milan has decided to provide weekly food assistance to elderly and vulnerable citizens until the pandemic process is over. In this crisis environment, the municipality of Milan has tried to fulfill its services within the framework of its powers, duties and responsibilities in order to meet local common needs and support citizens (https://www.comune.milano.it/ Access: 15.05.2021). In this context, they took initiative at the local level in the management of the pandemic process with the regulations issued and the funds established by metropolitan city governments and regional governments.

The struggle to control and return to normal life of the Covid-19 pandemic, which is still having its impact globally, continues at all levels from the international level to national policies and local units. Having a synergy at all levels, institutions acting in unity and controlling the epidemic is very important for normal life. Epidemics require the joint work and cohesion of all institutions, civil society and professional organizations, both globally and nationally. Therefore, the presence of strong corporate structures, compliance and awareness of collaboration will contribute to overcoming this difficult process with less damage. At this point, the services that each institution normally maintains, conducting it jointly with another institution will ensure stability in success. In this context, strategies for combating the covid-19 pandemic are case management, prevention of transmission and taking control measures and vaccination policy. In the management of the process, detection of cases, rapid isolation, and an effective surveillance system to prevent the spread of transmission are key.

As a result, in this painful process that the world is experiencing today, the attitude that neoliberal understanding does not recognize any alternative other than capital economics, which puts global capital before human beings, can be shown as the basis for the source of the problem. The fact that epidemics have a huge impact on humanity, living beings, the environment, social life, and the economy in all aspects is an answer to understandings that put economic order and growth ahead of everything else.

References

Bilgiç, V., (1998). Yerel Yönetimler, 21. Century Bookstore, Ankara.
Baccetti C., (2013). L'Ente Intermedio in Europa-Caratteri istituzionali e politici del governo locale di secondo livello in alcuni paesi europei (Belgio, Francia, Germania, Polonia, Regno Unito, Spagna e Italia), Alıntı: http://www.upinet.it/docs/contenuti/2013/03/RelazioncperAssembleaUPI-26-27%20VI.pdf, Access Tarihi: 01.12.2019.
Eryılmaz, B., (2010). Kamu Yönetimi: Düşünceler, Yapılar, Fonksiyonlar, Okutman Bookstore, Ankara.
Geray C., (1997). İtalya'da Yerel Yönetimler, Çağdaş Yerel Yönetimler Journal, S.6(1), 53-76.
Karabaş E., (1991). Avrupa Topluluğu Ülkelerinde Yerel ve Bölgesel Yönetimlerin Yapısı, Unpublished Doctoral Thesis, İstanbul Üniversitesi/ Sosyal Bilimler Enstitusü, İstanbul.
Koçak Y., (2013). Türkiye'de Yerel Yönetimler, Siyasal Bookstore, Ankara.

Küçük, H . (2019). Yerel Yönetim Sistemlerinde İtalya Örneği. Journal of Political Administrative and Local Studies, 2 (1), 1-26.

Marchetti G., (2010). Italian Regions and Local Authorities within the framework of a new Autonomist System, Perspectives on Federalism, Vol. 2, Issue 1.

Olivetti M., (2014). Centralization vs. Decentralization: The Current Trends in Italy, Korel Göymen ve Onur Sazlak (Ed.), Centralization Decentralization Debate Revisited, İstanbul.

Tortop, N., (1996). İtalya'da Yerel Yönetimlerin Yapısı ve Son Düzenlemeler, Çağdaş Yerel Yönetimler Journal, S.3 (5), 63-70.

Ulusoy, A. ve T., Akdemir, (2013). Mahalli İdareler: Teori-Uygulama-Maliye, 8. Baskı, Seçkin Bookstore, Ankara.

Ulusoy, A. ve T., Akdemir, (2001). Mahalli İdareler: Teori-Uygulama-Maliye, Seçkin Bookstore, Ankara.

The Municipality of Milan, (2020), https://www.comune.milano.it/ Access: 15.05.2021

WHO (World Health Organisation), https://covid19.who.int, Access: 07.05.2021.

Worldometer, https://www.worldometers.info, Access: 07.05.2021.

Our World in Data, https://ourworldindata.org, Access: 07.05.2021.

ECDC (European Centre for Disease Prevention and Control), https://www.ecdc.europa.eu/en/publications-data/download-data-hospital-and-icu-admission-rates-and-current-occupancy-covid-19, Access: 07.05.2021.

Our World in Data, https://ourworldindata.org/grapher/public-transport-covid?region=Europe, Access: 07.05.2021.

Our World in Data, https://ourworldindata.org/covid-vaccinations?country=ITA, Access: 07.05.2021.

John Hopkins University, https://coronavirus.jhu.edu/map.html, Access: 07.05.2021.

Governo Italiano Presidenza del Consiglio dei Ministri, https://www.governo.it/it/articolo/domande-frequenti-sulle-misure-adottate-dal-governo, Access: 04.05.2021.

Governo Italiano Presidenza del Consiglio dei Ministri, https://www.governo.it/it/articolo/domande-frequenti-sulle-misure-adottate-dal-governo/15638#zone, Access: 04.05.2021.

TC Ticaret Bakanlığı, https://ticaret.gov.tr/yurtdisi-teskilati/avrupa/italya/ulke-profili/kovid-19-gelismeleri, Access: 05.05.2021.

Ministero degli Affari Esteri e della Cooperazione Internazionale, https://www.esteri.it/mae/en/ministero/normativaonline/decreto-iorestoacasa-domande-frequenti/focus-cittadini-italiani-in-rientro-dall-estero-e-cittadini-stranieri-in-italia.html, Access: 04.05.2021.

Gazetta Ufficiale Della Repubblica Italiana, https://www.gazzettaufficiale.it/eli/id/2020/10/13/20A05563/sg, Access: 04.05.2021.

Gazetta Ufficiale Della Repubblica Italiana, https://www.gazzettaufficiale.it/dettaglioArea/12, Access: 04.05.2021.

Accesso diretto ai siti web delle Regioni, http://www.regioni.it/regioni-online/, Access: 04.05.2021.

Regione Lombardia, https://www.regione.lombardia.it/wps/portal/istituzionale/HP/coronavirus/misure, Access: 04.05.2020.

Regione Campania, http://www.regione.campania.it/regione/it/la-tua-campania/coronavirus-kyxz/ordinanze-del-presidente-della-regione-campania, Access: 04.05.2021.

TC Adalet Bakanlığı, (1948 İtalya Anayasası). http://www.adalet.gov.tr/duyurular/2011/eylul/anayasalar/ulkeana/pdf/10-%C4%B0TALYA%20319-354.pdf, Access: 01.05.2021.

GENDER AND CLIMATE CHANGE

Tefide KIZILDENİZ[*]
Cansu ÇİFTÇİ[**]
Alea LAIDLAW[***]

1. Climate Change Linkages with Agriculture, Food Security and Gender Dimension

Food security enables people, that have different financial, sociable, and physical conditions, access to suitable, dependable, and nourishing food to continue their not only active but also healthy lives (FAO, 2002, 2013). Understanding food security is important because it reduces the global hunger levels associated with malnutrition. Agriculture, which provides basic food and raw materials, is essential for sustainable food security (Umesha et. al., 2018).

Agriculture is not only making a significant contribution to food use by increasing the amount and variety of food but also supports people who live in rural areas dependent on agriculture for their livelihoods. In rural areas, individuals meet their daily nutritional needs through agricultural production and mutually maintain a stable income (Mozumdar, 2012). Insufficient financial resources limit regular access to food, so the resulting food insecu-

---

[*] Niğde Ömer Halisdemir University, Faculty of Agricultural Sciences and Technologies, Biosystem Engineering Department, 51240, Niğde, TURKEY, ORCID Code: 0002-5627-1307, Corresponding author: tkizildeniz@ohu.edu.tr.

[**] Niğde Ömer Halisdemir University, Faculty of Agricultural Sciences and Technologies, Agricultural Genetic Engineering Department, 51240, Niğde, TURKEY, ORCID Code: 0003-4771-7765.

[***] Faculty of the Earth and Environmental Science Department, Science in Society Program, Wesleyan University, Connecticut, USA, Edinburgh University, faculty of the Global Academy of Agriculture and Food Security, Edinburgh, The UK, ORCID Code: 0001-8492-7855.

rity increases the risk of many chronic diseases such as diabetes. In the case of loss of food safety, people cannot reach a sufficient nutrient amount and quality, so this negatively affects their health (Myers, 2019). For example, during the global pandemic the spread of the virus may affect the livelihood of individuals, and subsequently food security, specifically in countries that meet their access to food and economic income through the agricultural sector. On the other hand, since people in countries struggling with hunger have limited access to sufficient nutrients, if serious diseases such as COVID-19 spread in this region, the immunity of individuals will be insufficient and the damage to the health system will be increased (Siche, 2020). Food security provides individuals with continuous access to nutrients with sufficient nutrient content for a healthy life. In such situations that affect the world, the continuity of the agricultural sector is of great importance, especially for the people of rural life who have low income and earn their financial income through agriculture. From this perspective, the continuity of agriculture is of critical importance for the concept of "unlimited access to food" included in the definition of food security.

On the other hand, the low productivity in agriculture adversely affects food security, when it is coupled with population growth. Agricultural developments are important to ensure sustainable food access and improve nutrition under all financial, sociable, and physical conditions in food security. For the sustainability of food security, in societies whose main sources of income depend on agricultural products, economic development and preventing malnutrition are directly proportional to agricultural developments. Therefore, increasing agricultural production and productivity is an important factor to ensure food safety principles, especially in underdeveloped countries (Mozumdar, 2012).

Agriculture has important roles for food supply, which includes suitable, dependable, and nourishing in terms of food security. The first main role of production in food security is to supply adequate food. The capability of agriculture in meeting the food demand is directly related to the availability of sufficient food in food security. The global temperature increase has an impact on food security in rural areas as it affects agricultural production (Vermeulen et. al., 2012). The second is to provide access to the necessary reserves to consume sufficient food, and climate change causes unstable access to resources necessary to consume enough food.

Although the increased amount of carbon dioxide can increase the productivity of the crop according to the type of plants, this situation also causes the plants to be exposed to various environmental stressors such as water amount, mineral balance, air pollution are taken into account (McCarthy et. al., 2001). Although the increased amount of carbon dioxide in the atmosphere can increase the yield of certain species, this increase in yield may not positively affect the nutritional values in the obtained product. For instance, the protein content of some crops has decreased inversely with increasing atmospheric carbon dioxide (Schmidhuber and Tubiello, 2007; McCarthy et. al., 2001).

The increasing concentration of greenhouse gases, which causes high atmospheric temperatures, creates the risk of losing access to food with water scarcity. For instance, if agricultural workers do not get enough food in a rural area with irregular rainfall, there will be no stable access to food. Whereas, food security covers the stable access of individuals to food in all financial, sociable, and physical conditions (Mozumdar, 2012). Changes in environmental factors, such as temperature and precipitation, affect agriculture that is required food availability, thus it also affects ensuring sustainable food security.

Besides, climate change may cause infectious diseases by blocking access to healthy food and water, and change the condition of efficient use of food in food security (Schmidhuber and Tubiello, 2007). Declining food diversity as a result of global climate change restricts the continuity of access to nutritious food. When we consider the psychological effects such as depression that may occur as a result of food insecurity, climate change affects the health of individuals not only physically but also mentally in this way. For example, while deficient intake of nutrients as a result of increased food insecurity leads to HIV, the increased psychological depression caused by food insecurity is another factor that increases the likelihood of disease transmission (Weiser et. al., 2011).

In addition, the increase in food demand with changing climatic conditions will affect the global economy (McCarthy et. al., 2001). Another dimension in food security will be accessing sufficient resources in order to obtain food. Every man, woman, and child has physical and economic access to nutritionally adequate and safe food in the right for food (FAO, 2010; Neven, 2014). In the agricultural sector, rural women have a fundamental role in all stages of food production, and they are also concerned with access to and use of food. In agricultural activities, women have roles such as weeding, harvesting, carrying water, and selecting seeds. Men spend more time in soil preparation and to access financial resources such as loans for land expenses. Post-harvest women manage their food supply, increasing food availability until the next harvest season. Additionally, gender affects the food security of the household as women are responsible for the selection, processing, and preparation of products for a balanced diet (UNEP, 2017). When crop shortages occur as a result of climatic conditions, men culturally often migrate to find jobs in another region. In this case, women have to struggle with the sustainability of the effective use of food (OHCHR, 2010). Thus, gender inequalities need to be addressed for stable availability, access, and use of adequate food in food security.

The main factors of food security are availability, access, use, and stability of sufficient food. Agriculture that provides basic food affects food security in terms of availability of sufficient and regular nutritious food. Environmental changes that occur with increasing carbon dioxide concentration in the atmosphere harm agriculture and healthy food production. On the other hand, the gender factor determines the sharing of duties, especially among the rural people who meet their livelihood and food need through agriculture. Climate change affects both agricultural production and the determination of gender roles. In short, to address malnutrition in all its forms, all situations that may affect food security, such as climate change, the gender factor, and agricultural activities, should be taken into account.

2. Gender-Sensitive Strategies in The Sustainable Agriculture Towards Climate Change

The concept of gender differs according to the responsibilities and roles determined in cultural differentiation. Since men and women play interrelated but fundamentally different roles, there are gender-based responsibility differences in the division of labor. The gender-sensitive approach is to try to ensure equal opportunities and participation, taking into account the consequences for both men and women and boys and girls in the policies and programs organized (European Commission, 1998). This approach, which deals with the situations that may arise with gender differences, aims to increase gender equality. For this reason, situations where gender roles are different, such as the agriculture sector, and areas where there is still inequality of opportunity, such as education systems, can be developed with gender-sensitive approach strategies. For example, the role of women in the regular supply of households with food cannot be ignored and this is a gender-sensitive issue.

Many regional, national, and international plans, strategies, and training have been organized in line with gender sensitivity. For example, Agenda 21 is the international agreement adopted in 1922, which aims to provide governments with various changes regarding women's participation in sustainable development. Another example of gender-sensitive approaches, The World Sustainable Development Summit (WSSD) Implementation Plan, adopted in 2002, supports gender-based equality of opportunity and access of girls and women to areas that contribute to the improvement of well-being, such as health, education, and financial resources (Corat, et al., 2009).

Variation in access to services, resources, and opportunities depending on the gender difference thereby causing low productivity in agriculture and thus affects other factors such as food security and economic conditions. Women's control and access to various resources should be increased in order that contribute to the increase of agricultural production. At this point, all situations that have direct or indirect effects on each other should be considered. In addition to support such as land use planning, access to necessary financial resources; health, social security, ensuring adequate access to resources such as water, electricity, transportation and all other factors necessary for similar living conditions should be evaluated. Thus, positive developments are observed in processes such as the well-being and nutritional needs of the household and child support for education (Dookie et. al., 2013).

Although the contribution of women to agriculture varies according to countries, regions, and age factors; women have various responsibilities in agriculture, such as production, harvesting, marketing, and the use of food obtained in the diet of the household. While especially women living in rural areas have to manage many roles at the same time, unfortunately, their access to resources is generally limited compared to men. Developing gender-sensitive strategies are very important in the agricultural sector when considering women's contribution to food security, agricultural production, and the economy. Generally, women cannot produce independently from men, the crops are obtained by a common workforce and different roles. As an example, men are involved in the cultivation of the soil, while women are involved in the selection and cultivation of the seed variety, together the two take part in the harvest of the crop. However, women generally take part in every stage of the food cycle stages, albeit for different periods. In addition to food production, women have a role in animal products such as animal feeding, milking, egg collection, and marketing of these products. Financial resources, such as loans, to move to large enterprises commonly provide more support to male producers. On the other hand, women's access to economic support remains limited in most regions. Due to the lack of time, the working time of women who are also responsible for elderly people and children in the household is decreasing. In a gender-sensitive approach, while developing strategies based on gender roles, it is necessary to analyze all the responsibilities of women and men depending on the age factor and regional differences (Raney et. al., 2011).

According to the research, which includes the results of the Green Revolution on women farmers living in India, for the applicability of technological developments, they should be sensitive to concepts such as resource, need, and participation in different social conditions. Agricultural developments must be made gender-sensitive, because farming women, who are often ignored, play a role in both production and household income. Women have valuable knowledge not only on the production of food, but also on the storage of food, and the selection of seed types, plant parts, fruits, and spices for the processing and preparation of nutritious foods by several years of experience and traditional knowledge transfer. Ensuring that women, who have more responsibilities than men, have access to improvements in agricultural practices is also important for sustainability in agriculture. Unfortunately, women's participation in programs and training to improve agriculture is limited. The limited access to these supports increases the workload of women together with gender roles. For this reason, gender-sensitive strategies in agricultural sustainability are essential for the Green Revolution to have a positive impact on gender equality (Singh et al., 2010).

Climate-smart agriculture (CSA) is an approach that supports sustainability in agriculture and aims to increase agricultural production to maintain food security in the change of climate conditions. In the developed agricultural development plans, the climate-smart agriculture (CSA) approach develops gender-sensitive strategies. CSA covers applications such as irrigation, the efficient use of fertilizers, the development of new varieties to increase yield, the cultivation of plants that are tolerant to various stress factors, and the storage of animal manure. In these practices, gender equality based strategies are developed considering not only changing climatic conditions but also sociocultural differences (WBG, FAO & IFAD, 2015).

Due to the impact of women on agricultural production, climate change particularly affects women living in rural areas due to women's more pervasive in production. Gender-sensitive support is an important approach in development plans for the sustainability of agriculture under climate change because women and men have different ease of access to resources such as financial support (UNEP, 2017).

The Gender Analysis Tool in Agricultural Policy (GAPo) was developed by FAO as a gender-sensitive tool to support the needs and opportunities in the agricultural sector equally among women and men. GAPo aims to support women by taking gender equality into account in agricultural policies, thus helping stakeholders and national governments with a gender-sensitive approach to policies. In its policies, GAPo emphasizes areas such as agricultural research, resource access, financial services that can have an impact on the livelihoods of women in rural areas with diverse roles. Besides, it acknowledges that gender equality should be considered in every policy (Kaaria and Villani, 2016).

CGIAR Climate Change, Agriculture and Food Security Research Program (CCAFS) places emphasis on gender-sensitive systems in agricultural development strategies as a result of climate change. It addresses gender roles and relationships for adaptation to changing conditions and increased production by managing the negative consequences of climate change. Activities that empower women in changing climate conditions have an impact on both productivity and food security. One of the goals of CCAFS research is to address the effects of gender difference, so it is determined to allocate some of its budget for social differentiation research such as age, gender, and well-being (CGIAR, 2011).

A Climate Change and Gender Action Plan (ccGAP: Bangladesh) has been prepared for Bangladesh, a country that is highly affected by the negative influences of climate change. Approximately half of the population in Bangladesh consists of women who are interested in the agricultural sector. Thus, climate change both negatively affects agricultural development activities and makes women vulnerable. There are equal gender rights in the Bangladesh Constitution. BCCSAP also addressed the needs of women and children in its action plan for developing gender-sensitive climate change strategies (ccGAP: Bangladesh, 2013).

Development of Sustainable Agriculture in the Pacific (DSAP) is a project started in 2003 by the Secretariat of the Pacific Community (SPC) to improve agricultural systems at the country level. Gender-sensitive strategies have been developed within the scope of the project. As a result, both male and female farmers have benefited from reducing the effects of climate change (Corat, 2009).

Women have roles in different stages of agricultural production, economy, and food security. Agricultural problems caused by climate change can change gender-related responsibilities and subsequently harm women's roles. Agricultural development plans, projects, and training that emerge to reduce the harmful effects of climate change on agriculture and food production should be gender-sensitive. To date, many gender-sensitive sustainable agriculture strategies have been developed by addressing regional differences, gender equality, and age factors. In this way, continuity in agricultural production and access to food can be achieved.

3. Gender Mainstreaming in Climate Change Adaptation and Mitigation

The process of evaluating the results of policies, programs, and actions planned in any field to achieve gender equality in terms of men and women is the mainstreaming of gender. It is a strategy that combines every stage of policies and programs, such as planning, implementation, and evaluation, to be realized with the perspectives and experiences of both women and men. Gender-based issues vary across circumstances, countries, and regions. Gender mainstreaming takes a gender-sensitive approach that evaluates the priorities, roles, and needs of the genders while taking this into account. The use of gender equality in all policies and programs evaluates the role and needs differences in women and men, as well as the effects of participation and decision-making processes. Gender mainstreaming strategies aim to prevent problems by addressing the effects of gender inequality on the opportunities provided and their consequences. In this way, it ensures fair and effective achievement of sustainable development goals in economic, political, social, and all other areas (Corat, 2009; FAO, 2017).

Adaptation to climate change aims to reduce the negative effects that occur in order to adapt to changing climatic conditions and to benefit from the conditions such as season extension (NASA, 2021).

Mitigation in climate change aims to reduce human activities that release greenhouse gases, the use of fossil fuels, thereby increasing the atmospheric temperature. In this way, these preventative measures are aimed in preventing the impact of climate change on sustainable agricultural production and economic development by balancing the greenhouse gas level (NASA, 2021).

Climate change has a greater negative impact on women than on men. For this reason, all situations should be evaluated in order to achieve the desired targets in climate change adaptation strategies. Gender differences should be taken into account in adaptation strategies to reduce risks in changing conditions (Pearl et al., 2009).

Women and men do not have equal access to and use of resources. Therefore, women are more vulnerable to climate change. In poor communities that depend on natural resources, women, children and the elderly suffer the most when access to resources becomes difficult (Corat, 2009). Gender differences should be considered in the measures taken to reduce greenhouse gas emissions and mitigate the effects of climate change. The gender role difference has made women more knowledgeable about transportation, energy, food production, and natural resources. Because of these role differences, the gender factor should be evaluated in order to achieve the goals regarding climate change. For example, engaging in activities for women in the use of natural resources such as solar energy will directly serve the purpose of the climate change mitigation process due to the distribution of roles (Habtezion, 2016).

On the other hand, studies on the role of women in agricultural production have shown, for example, that farmers' productivity increases when women are provided with equal opportunities with men in Kenya. In another study in Africa, it was shown that agricultural production yield increased as a result of increased gender equality. Access to water resources can be considered in gender mainstreaming strategies. Water use, pollution, and how it will be supplied in the future can be analyzed by considering the purposes of using this resource by men and women (United Nations, 2002).

For example, in Vietnam, it is a common view that women are physiologically weak, and there is wide gap in gender equality. In addition, depending on the age, weak individuals are defined as feminine and their responsibilities are determined accordingly. It is thought that women and elderly people should work in light jobs in communities. Men can move freely, so they can communicate with other communities, but women are limited in this regard. Differences in the division of labor and movement reduce women's opportunities to fight against climate change. This situation additionally affects women's ability to adapt to climate change. Vietnam is heavily affected by climate change whereby adverse weather events such as floods are frequent and severe. For the sustainability of agricultural production, it is essential to consider the gender factor in climate change adaptation and mitigation policies (Ylipaa et al., 2019).

Climate change has effects on several areas, like the economy, agriculture sector, food security, and health. It affects all countries in different ways depending on regions, communities, gender, and occupation. Women are more sensitive to climate change than men cause of their natural vulnerability. Adaptation to variable conditions under global warming highly varies across gender. Therefore, situations, that have a relationship between climate change such as, mitigation, policies, and adaptation, must be focused on gender factors (Aguilar, 2010).

Women are disadvantaged within their limited rights, access, and resources therefore making them vulnerable to climate change. The participation of women in these processes is important in climate-based adaptation policies. In particular, the agricultural sector is easily affected by changing environmental conditions and women have the role of food producers. Changes in climate affect important situations such as food security and water use. At this point, gender-sensitive approaches should be developed for the welfare of the household and the continuity of the diet. As an example, women from the Keur Moussa community in Senegal maintain agricultural production by building canals to control erosion when land is flooded (UNDP and GGCA, 2009).

Another example of the importance of gender-sensitive strategies, were the death rates after the Southeast Asia tsunami that broke out in December 2004. In such natural disasters, men have a better chance of survival as they are taught to swim. In countries such as India, Sri Lanka, and Indonesia, it has increased the risk of death for women vulnerable to disaster (Maguire and Hagan, 2007). Gender sensitivity should be ensured in all activities, programs, and projects in order to prevent similar consequences in floods that may occur as a result of climate change. This can be beneficial in terms of both demography and sustainability due to gender-based role distribution. Since women are more likely to be present in regions where climate-related risks arise, the risk of women in these physical positions increases (Chauhan and Vinaya Kumar, 2016).

During pregnancy and post-pregnancy period, women become sensitive to nutrition. This affects them more negatively against nutritional deficiencies in climate change (Chauhan and Vinaya Kumar, 2016). Looking at the economic condition of the sexes in rural areas, men predominantly have higher incomes and have broader access to resources such as natural resources and financial support. For example, according to FAO (UNDP and GGCA, 2009), the proportion of women who own the land among Thai and Nepalese farmers is less than 10 percent. Unfortunately, women with lower incomes are also located in areas where natural disaster risk is high (Chauhan and Vinaya Kumar, 2016).

Inequality of educational opportunities prevents women from accessing communication and information, preventing women from responding to early warnings in possible crisis situations, droughts, and floods. Considering political situations, again, women are unlikely to access representation and power. This situation differentiates the vulnerability of the sexes to the risks posed by climate change. Another obstacle is the problem of women's access to financial resources in the agricultural workforce. According to a study conducted by the World Bank in 141 countries, many of these countries restrict women's access to financial resources due to gender differences. Unfortunately, it also puts women at a financial disadvantage in their climate change adaptation initiatives. Additionally, women's lack of access to policies and activities weakens them in decision-making and implementation processes. Subsequently, emerging social principles limit women's ability to avoid disasters. In other words, the defense capabilities of the genders are different in adverse scenarios predicted to occur with climate change (Chauhan and Vinaya Kumar, 2016). Since women are likely to be subjected to violence and sexual assault after disasters, women may avoid using shelters due to emerging anxiety (Maguire and Hagan, 2007). On the other hand, in some disaster situations, men, who are seen as stronger by society, lose their lives by attempting to rescue without any precaution. As an example, it can be shown that in Hurricane Mitch that occurred in Central America, the deaths of men increased because they took fewer precautions against possible risks (Maguire and Hagan, 2007).

Considering the importance of the decisions made by women for sustainable consumption, the impact of women on carbon sequestration due to their role in forestry, and women's responsibilities in providing energy resources, strategies based on gender should be widespread in mitigation of climate change (Karlsson, 2009). In climate change mitigation activities, nature protection and afforestation activities in forestry are important to increase greenhouse gas capture. Therefore, gender-based roles, access opportunities, knowledge, and skills differences should be taken into account in the study objectives in this field. In the forestry sector, the duty of women may be to plant and grow seedlings, to collect products for household burning, and to meet food and healing products. Men, on the other hand, are more interested in products such as timber used for commercial purposes (Karlsson, 2009). The Chipko Movement, organized in the Himalayas, revealed that women brought change through afforestation efforts. These activities both benefited in the case of landslides and solved the feed and fuel problem. At the same time, with this movement, the region has been banned from cutting trees and sensitive policies have been started regarding ecology (Karlsson, 2009).

Support in Karnataka, India is an example of gender-sensitive projects in agroforestry. In the project implemented by Women For Sustainable Development [WSD], while both genders are supported, restrictions on women and their shortcomings in the decision-making process have come to light. Providing equal opportunities for the sexes, benefits have been provided to carbon capture and fruit production with mango, tamarind, and jackfruit trees on the land (Karlsson, 2009). Since the use of transport vehicles is not common in rural areas, greenhouse gas emissions are generally low in these regions. However, it is common to use wood and coal for heating, cooking, and lighting in these regions of countries such as Africa. Men are typically more interested in plumbing and thermal insulation. Women are responsible for providing fuel and can therefore have a significant impact on greenhouse gas reduction efforts (Karlsson, 2009).

Sustainable consumption, which takes into account the environmental conditions, economy, population, etc., and the production of products, is affected by the gender factor. For example, women are more involved in sustainable consumption than men, as they attach more importance to organic food, energy efficiency, and recycling. In order to increase women's participation in water management and decrease women's vulnerability in disasters such as floods, a gender-sensitive approach was followed in the water basin management training program (Asteria et. al., 2018).

In the activity carried out in Indonesia, a gender-sensitive strategy was followed by ensuring the participation of women in basin management. In the cities of Jakarta and Tasikmalaya, where flood disasters are common, the emphasis has been placed on women's participation in watershed management activities. Through training programs, women have been provided with the ability to manage events according to the type of basin. With the water basin management activities of women, precautions were taken for the cutting of trees around the basin, and greening and cleaning were provided (Asteria et. al., 2018).

There are various developments showing that gender-sensitive financing supports will be in climate change. After the 14th Conference of the Parties (COP 14) of the United Nations Framework Convention on Climate Change (UNFCCC), a gender-based approach has been adopted in economic climate support. For example, in the Green Climate Fund (GCF) it has been undertaken to take gender sensitivity into account. The supports in the Sustainable Development Goals (SDGs) have shown that there will be gender-sensitive strategies. Gender differences have been involved in Nationally Appropriate Mitigation Actions (NAMAs) until 2020, under the UNFCCC (United Nations Framework Convention on Climate Change). Later climate change measures from 2020 to 2030 included a gender-sensitive approach to planning (Zusman et al., 2016).

Participatory Research in Climate Change and Agriculture has been developed to identify gender-related vulnerabilities in climate change and to include gender differences in the scope of implemented projects. In adaptation and mitigation strategies, the sensitivity of different genders, differences in access to resources, and the effects of climate change policies on men and women have been observed. Analysis in line with the gender toolbox is facilitated gender-sensitive research in climate change. One of the goals of this tool is to create data analysis that explains the attitudes of different genders (men and women) in strengthening food security and adapting to climate change (Cramer et. al., 2017).

Increasing access to renewable energy sources in reducing greenhouse gas emissions can be beneficial in combating energy deprivation, given women's needs. Women's responsibilities in energy management can have a positive impact on renewable energy production and expansion (IUCN Global Gender Office, USAID, and EGI, 2016).

Recommendations to reduce greenhouse gas emissions The concept of gender is taken into account in projects proposed in the targets or results of Nationally Appropriate Mitigation Actions (NAMAs). A gender-sensitive approach has been adopted in activities such as increasing the efficiency of biomass fuels (IUCN Global Gender Office, USAID, and EGI, 2016). In some of the Low Emission Development Strategies (LEDs) that support low carbon-emission economic growth in the face of climate change, it has committed to identifying the vulnerability of women to climate change (IUCN Global Gender Office, USAID, and EGI, 2016).

Gender mainstreaming is the process of evaluating the results by considering gender differences in all kinds of policies, programs and actions that are desired to be implemented. It tries to solve the problems related to gender inequality by evaluating the changing situations according to countries and regions together with the factors of women, men and age. Thus, it ensures sustainable achievement of development goals in all areas.

Climate change adaptation policies aim to reduce the negative effects caused by increasing atmospheric carbon dioxide. The purpose of climate change mitigation efforts is to minimize the emission of greenhouse gases that cause rising temperatures in the atmosphere. Although climate change affects all of humanity; the adaptation of men and women to new conditions is not the same due to reasons such as access to resources, inequality of opportunity, and differences in role distribution. Therefore, it is necessary to evaluate the gender factor in order to achieve the climate change related targets. Gender is a fundamental dimension to climate change mitigation strategies and needs to be placed within the forefront of decision making.

4. Gender-Sensitive Strategies on Transfer and Development of Technology

In society, especially in rural areas, the responsibilities of women and men are different and the prescribed roles cause each gender to have different needs. In order to ensure equal access to resources and opportunities by eliminating gender inequalities, the processes that address the gender dimension are gender-sensitive strategies.

Gender equality, as expressed by UNESCO, takes into account the needs, interests and priorities of both girls and boys and men and women in different communities. Aiming to promote the right to education, the Education Program promotes gender equality for access to education and equal access to opportunities. While women and men are the users of technology, regardless of gender, in technology, machines have been operated primarily by men and women have been encouraged to work in the field of engineering in recent years (Rathgeber, 2009). UNESCO is sensitive to gender equality by supporting women in natural sciences and social sciences policies in various ways (UNFPA and WEDO, 2009) and also with priority gender equality action plan (2014-2021) (UNESCO, 2014).

The future state of food security is of great concern as crops are highly sensitive to temperatures rising, atmospheric carbon dioxide and precipitation variation. While informing the policies and the public, it is essential for the agricultural sector to reveal the impacts of climate change and the adaptation options that can be achieved with technology in order to reduce these impacts. Various models and statistical data are used in order to predict the effect of climate change on the yield of future crops (Aggarwal et. al., 2019). In a study conducted by the effects of climate change for the 2010-2039, time period was evaluated in a national context and analyzed in wheat, corn and rice. The results demonstrated the importance of technology in preventing predicted crop loss. In climate change, which will increase food insecurity in various regions, the spread of technological developments and providing suitable conditions will be an important factor (Aggarwal et. al., 2019).

Predominately, agricultural productivity in developing countries is low. Therefore, it is critical to develop and disseminate new technologies in the agricultural sector for climate change mitigation and adaptation in specific areas where food insecurity and fragility are high (Rathgeber, 2009). Climate change mitigation and adaptation for resource use reduction, increased food production and food production under varying conditions are imperative in agriculture. Agricultural technology is linked to opportunities for water use efficiency and greenhouse gas reduction (Lybbert and Sumner, 2012). Interconnected agriculture, food security and climate change require technological innovations and incentives to increase productivity (Vermeulen et.al., 2012).

Technology needs to be included in the activities in the climate change mitigation and adaptation process. In addition, technologies developed should be gender sensitive, taking into account the needs of both men and women. Women and men differ in access to technological information and tools, educational opportunities, and social prejudices to which they are exposed. There are also cultural differences in roles and opportunities between the genders and women generally lack income. As an example of this, in some communities, men manage water resources, and women use water from remaining of animal consumption, not taps, to bring water to the household (Rathgeber, 2009).

Strategies for gender neutral technology have different consequences for men and women to adapt and mitigate climate change. Considering the evolving differences, environmental education around climate change should be disseminated. The technology used by both genders should take into account the preferences and circumstances of women and men. Technologies are beneficial for both genders and increase productivity, and gender conditions are important to achieving the goal, especially in technologies with women as a priority. There are technologies that are generally designed by ignoring women's needs, time, labor and capital. While male farmers benefit from new technologies in the agricultural sector of developing countries, it becomes difficult for them to communicate with women farmers cause of socio-cultural restrictions. As a result, male farmers benefit from the introduction of new technologies, but female farmers cannot learn about these technologies. When the role of women in the agriculture sector is evaluated, this situation has a very negative effect (Rathgeber, 2009).

Gender being a social construct and although there is a basic biological foundation around sex, the ways in which gender is enacted is fundamentally cultural and socially imposed. Therefore, gender-related needs variability should first be accepted for instance, different technology needs, and evaluation of their studies. As another example, the processing of products in the agricultural sector is the responsibility of women in many rural societies. It would be appropriate to invest in the production of tools that facilitate this laborious and time-consuming job and increase productivity in a short time and to develop this new technology. Women and men have different access to financial resources and information, as well as the roles they devote to time, and the conditions of the gender of the application's user must be taken into account in technology needs analysis (Rathgeber, 2009).

It is difficult for women to access resources that enable the distribution of technical information such as agricultural extension systems. For example, male individuals may not pass on the technical knowledge they have learned to women in the household. Especially if women have their own lands other than the land of their husband, the man may not share the new information with the woman. For this reason, it is important to have channels that can directly transfer information to women in agricultural extension systems and to spread them. In other words, the concept of gender should also be taken into account in climate change in agricultural extension systems. While transferring information in this way, women's learning techniques should also be taken into account in presentations containing technical information on climate change (Rathgeber, 2009).

In the dissemination of technology, it is important to have a suitable environment as well as the correct determination of gender differences and how information will be disseminated. It is important that all stakeholders, such as public institutions and organizations, private sector and organizations, participate in technology transfer. Women should be able to be present at all stakeholders and express their views. In some societies, it is considered disrespectful for women to speak in front of men. Considering these and similar situations, it may be appropriate to talk to women in a private way (Rathgeber, 2009).

Likewise, equality of opportunity should be provided to both genders in terms of technology dissemination, such as information, education and participation in jobs. Women should be supported in accessing opportunities and their participation in services such as financial and education should be increased. Technology transfer strategies should be organized in a gender-sensitive way by making the necessary analysis, considering the demands and needs differences, determining the priorities (Rathgeber, 2009).

There have been several technologies adapted for gender-sensitive strategies and approaches. One example of a successful gender-sensitive approach was 'The Rapid Gender Capacity Needs Assessment', implemented in Bhutan in 2013 in partnership with UNDP (UN Women, 2021). The assessment involved an in-depth gendered stakeholder analysis which highlighted particular gender inequality within the transportation, waste, and housing industries. Training workshops across these sectors were conducted regularly and were built around long-term contingency planning, addressing the gender gaps, and enabling accessible entrance points within these industries. Equal gender representation was maintained and regulated across the processes and this resulted in clear and pragmatic emission goals which involved the overarching scope, objective, and timeline. Since the global COVID-19 pandemic has caused an increase in remote learning and branches of income, the technologies could be moved onto a digital database.

Another clear example of a gender-sensitive approach was the Mitigation of Climate Change in Agriculture (MICCA) which was overseen by the Food and Agriculture Organization of the United

Nations (FAO, 2021). Agriculture was recognized as an economically viable and secure avenue to reduce greenhouse gas emissions, while maintaining a consistent and nutritiously viable yield. One methodology to increase carbon sinks in developing countries was through online community platforms, specifically through courses and group training sessions. By centralizing gender within climate smart agriculture (CSA), climate change adaptation and mitigation were highlighted and brought to the forefront of national stakeholders and localized farmer long term objectives. Viewing climate change adaptation strategies from a purely carbon emission model fundamentally bypasses the socio-cultural undercurrent of the entire system management. Climate change can only be addressed through simple individual actions, localized knowledge, and a breath of shared interdisciplinary discourse. The circulation of knowledge and technological strategies can then be fully implemented to combat food security and economic disparity.

Gender-sensitive mitigation technologies are aimed at providing equal access and representation both around the implementation and continuous monitoring efforts to ensure holistic and sustainable design. Climate change technologies have been shown to drastically improve yields, predict weather patterns, and protect local economies. In order to support ecofeminism within the context of the Anthropocene and agriculture environmental stressors, an in-depth gender analysis and women's engagement and participation needs to be prioritized. Addressing gender inequalities and inequities in the context of adaptation and resilience means developing an understanding of the different ways in which distinct socio-economic groups are affected by and are responding to climatic changes. According to the UNEP DTU Partnership in collaboration with UN environment, women are more dependent on natural resources for their livelihood than men (UNEP DTU Partnership, UN Environmental, and GEF, 2018). Subsequently, women become agents of social change at a grassroots and local community level by enacting conservation efforts and sustainable agricultural practices. Therefore, increasing female representation in political advocacy directly leads to an increased responsiveness for climate change mitigation strategies. Women are substantially more effected by decreasing yields and biomass productivity as climate change continues to be detrimental for rural economies.

Gender sensitive strategies are processes that take into account the different roles, responsibilities and access to opportunities of women and men, and that care about their needs and preferences in order to ensure equal access to the gender. The agricultural sector is an area that is directly sensitive to climate change, and new technological developments in processes such as adaptation to climate change and adaptation are tools to reach the target. As in other areas, although both genders benefit from technology, societies have limited access to technology and technical knowledge. Gender-related barriers should be considered in developing strategies for accessing technological resources. At the same time, client-oriented technologies should be developed and disseminated, taking into account the variable needs depending on gender. Additionally, unfortunately, women's access to technical information may be dependent on men. In order to eliminate this situation, dissemination activities should be made sensitive to gender according to women's access problems. Add sentence here about what some of the access problems may be- financial burden, family responsibility, social standards or social constructs of female behavior, Presentations on climate change adaptation, mitigation and technologies that women can understand can be made in media sources such as radio and television.

5. Gender Mainstreaming in Mechanisms of Climate Change Financing

Developing countries face a major challenge in situations such as irregular rainfall and frequent natural disasters are caused by climate change. Usually women and the poor feel these impacts most severely. These countries need financial resources to cope with climate change. In addition, it should be taken into account that both women and men are affected differently by climate change. Therefore, in a gender-sensitive manner financial resources and strategies to be developed accordingly (UN Women, 2021) Various national and international initiatives in climate change mitigation and adaptation strategies have resulted in actions at the financial level. Resources, technologies, and services require a serious financial resource for developed and developing countries to achieve the necessary strategic goals (Williams and Conze, 2009).

Climate change adaptation, mitigation targets and technologies for this should be structured in a special way in line with the difference of development levels (Williams and Conze, 2009). It is important to organize policies, plans and activities by evaluating the needs for the participation of both women and men in climate change in economic matters (UNFPA and WEDO, 2009). States that have developed in adapting to climate change have provided valuable economic support. These supports are usually provided by international development organizations. International organizations such as the United Nations Development Program, the World Bank, and the Organization for Economic Cooperation and Development have authorized states to implement and monitor climate change adaptation (Hall, 2017).

Women's adaptation to climate change differs from men in terms of gender and access to opportunities. Therefore, women often become more vulnerable to climate change, although it varies depending on society. Genders whose control over financial resources and the opportunity to access financial resources differ, and women's ability to adapt to climate change is linked to their access to these opportunities. Often the economic security of women is not taken into account when it comes to climate change within financing policies. Therefore, women should be encouraged to invest in projects and national carbon taxes that can benefit them directly. Climate change adaptation and greenhouse gas reduction financing projects in natural resource management and agricultural activities should be made compatible with women's participation (Williams and Conze, 2009).

Differential gender access to physical and social goods; differences such as time spent, education and income between men and women; When considering the changing society based on gender, household roles and workforce situations, it is necessary to empower women and increase their control over financial resources (Williams and Conze, 2009). The opportunity to access various resources such as water, energy and transportation is different in genders. For this reason, the rate of health, access to economic and social resources affects women's weakness in adapting to climate change (Williams and Conze, 2009). Climate change financing is essential for gender mainstreaming in order to generate economic incentives and to stabilize rural economies as climate change develops.

Climate change poses an expediting threat to food security and the agricultural sector specifically within rural communities in developing countries. The second UN Sustainable Development Goal is to "End hunger, achieve food security and improved nutrition, and promote sustainable agriculture." (Karttunen et. al., 2017). Women and men have different access to financial resources and information, as well as the roles they devote to time, and the conditions of the gender of the application's user must be taken into account in technology needs analysis (Rathgeber, 2009).

References

Aggarwal, P., Vyas, S., Thornton, P., Campbell, B. M., & Kropff, M. (2019). Importance of considering technology growth in impact assessments of climate change on agriculture. *Global Food Security*, 23, 41-48.

Aguilar, L. (2010) "Establishing the linkages between gender and climate change adaptation and mitigation." Gender and climate change: An introduction, ed. Irene Dankelman, 173-193.

Asteria, D., Herdiansyah, H., & Ni'mah, N. L. (2018). Gender sensitive education in watershed management to support environmental friendly city. In *IOP Conference Series: Earth and Environmental Science* (Vol. 126, No. 1, p. 012146). IOP Publishing.

ccGAP: Bangladesh (2013). Bangladesh Climate Change and Gender Action Plan. Ministry of Environment of Forest, Government of the People's Republic of Bangladesh. http://nda.erd.gov.bd/en/c/publication/climate-change-and-gender-action-plan-ccgap-2013 [accessed 8 May 2021]

CGIAR (The Consultative Group for International Agricultural Research) (2011). Research Program on Climate Change, Agriculture and Food Security CCAFS Program Plan. https://cgspace.cgiar.org/bitstream/handle/10568/10717/ccafs_program_plan_summary.pdf [accessed 10 May 2021]

Chauhan, N. B., & Vinaya Kumar H. M. (2016). Gender Responsive Climate Change Strategies for Sustainable Development. *Productivity, 57*(2).

Cramer, L., Huyer, S., Lavado, A., Loboguerrero Rodriguez, A. M., Martínez Barón, D., Nyasimi, M., ... & Wijk, M. T. V. (2017). Methods Proposed to Evaluate the Potential Impact of Climate Change on Food and Nutrition Security in Central America and the Dominican Republic.

Corat, S. G. (2009). Training manual on gender and climate change. Aguilar, L. (Main Author) Module 1: Gender and gender mainstreaming. The International Union for Conservation of Nature (IUCN) and the United Nations Development Programme (UNDP) in partnership with the Gender and Water Alliance, ENERGIA International Network on Gender and Sustainable Energy, United Nations Educational, Scientific and Cultural Organization (UNESCO), Food and Agriculture Organization (FAO) and the Women's Environment and Development Organization (WEDO) as part of the Global Gender and Climate Alliance (GGCA).

Corat, S. G., Duer, E. M., Anderson, C. L. and Sasvari, A. (2009). Training manual on gender and climate change. Aguilar, L. (Main Author) Module 2: International law instruments as a framework for mainstreaming gender in climate change. The International Union for Conservation of Nature (IUCN) and the United Nations Development Programme (UNDP) in partnership with the Gender and Water Alliance, ENERGIA International Network on Gender and Sustainable Energy, United Nations Educational, Scientific and Cultural Organization (UNESCO), Food and Agriculture Organization (FAO) and the Women's Environment and Development Organization (WEDO) as part of the Global Gender and Climate Alliance (GGCA).

Dookie, C., Lambrou, Y., & Petrics, H. (2013). *A tool for gender-sensitive agriculture and rural development policy and programme formulation: Guidelines for Ministries of Agriculture and FAO.* Food and Agriculture Organization of the United Nations (FAO).

European Commission (1998). Directorate-General for Employment, Industrial Relations, & Social Affairs. Unit V/D/. *One Hundred Words for Equality: A Glossary of Terms on Equality between Women and Men.*

FAO (Food and Agriculture Organization) (2002). The state of food insecurity in the world 2001 (No. 33). (Food and Agriculture Organization, Rome)

FAO (Food and Agriculture Organization) (2010). The state of food insecurity in the world: Addressing food insecurity in protracted crises. http://www.fao.org/3/i1683e/i1683e.pdf [accessed 27 March 2021]

FAO (Food and Agriculture Organization of the United States) (2013). *The state of food insecurity in the world, 2013: The multiple dimensions of food security.* Food and Agricultural Organization of the united Nations. http://www.fao.org/3/i1683e/i1683e00.htm [accessed 15 May 2021]

FAO (Food and Agriculture Organization) (2017). Gender mainstreaming and Human Rights based approach, Guidelines for Technical Officers. http://www.fao.org/3/a-i6808e.pdf [accessed 7 May 2021]

FAO (Food and Agriculture Organization) (2021). Mitigation of Climate Change in Agriculture (MICCA) Programme. http://www.fao.org/in-action/micca [accessed 7 May 2021]

Habtezion, S. (2016). Gender and climate change: Overview of linkages between gender and climate change. *New York: United Nations Development Programme.*

Hall, N. (2017). What is adaptation to climate change? Epistemic ambiguity in the climate finance system. *International Environmental Agreements: Politics, Law and Economics, 17*(1), 37-53.

IUCN Global Gender Office, USAID, and EGI (2016). Gender in Mitigation Actions. https://www.climatelinks.org/sites/default/files/asset/document/Gender%20In%20Mitigation%20Actions_April%202016.pdf [accessed 10 May 2021]

Kaaria, S. and Villani, C. (2016). The Gender in agricultural policies analysis Tool (GAPo). Food and Agriculture Organization of the United Nations (FAO). http://www.fao.org/documents/card/en/c/d3f88f54-5620-4b4e-ac40-130992be884e [accessed 11 April 2021]

Karlsson, G. (2009). Training manual on gender and climate change. Aguilar, L. (Main Author) Module 5: Gender-sensitive strategies for mitigation actions. International law instruments as a framework for mainstreaming gender in climate change. The International Union for Conservation of Nature (IUCN) and the United Nations Development Programme (UNDP) in partnership with the Gender and Water Alliance, ENERGIA International Network on Gender and Sustainable Energy, United Nations Educational, Scientific and Cultural Organization (UNESCO), Food and Agriculture Organization (FAO) and the Women's Environment and Development Organization (WEDO) as part of the Global Gender and Climate Alliance (GGCA).

Karttunen, A. K., Sisto, I., & Sadler, M. P. (2017). *How to integrate gender issues in climate-smart agriculture projects: training module* (No. 114441, pp. 1-72). The World Bank. http://www.fao.org/3/a-i6097e.pdf [accessed 7 May 2021]

Lybbert, T. J., & Sumner, D. A. (2012). Agricultural technologies for climate change in developing countries: Policy options for innovation and technology diffusion. *Food policy, 37*(1), 114-123.

Maguire, B., & Hagan, P. (2007). Disasters and communities: understanding social resilience. *Australian Journal of Emergency Management, The, 22*(2), 16-20.

McCarthy, J. J., Canziani, O. F., Leary, N. A., Dokken, D. J., & White, K. S. (Eds.). (2001). *Climate change 2001: impacts, adaptation, and vulnerability: contribution of Working Group II to the third assessment report of the Intergovernmental Panel on Climate Change* (Vol. 2). Cambridge University Press.

Mozumdar, L. (2012). Agricultural productivity and food security in the developing world. *Bangladesh Journal of Agricultural Economics*, 35(454-2016-36350), 53-69.

Myers, C. A. (2019). Understanding the importance of Food Insecurity among populations with diabetes. *Journal of diabetes and its complications*, 33(4), 340.

NASA (2021). Vital Signs of the Planet: Global Climate Change, Solutions, Mitigation and Adaptation. https://climate.nasa.gov/solutions/adaptation-mitigation/ [accessed 9 April 2021]

Neven, D. (2014). Developing sustainable food value chains Guiding principles. FAO (Food and Agriculture Organization of the United Nations.) http://www.fao.org/3/a-i3953e.pdf [accessed 1 April 2021]

OHCHR (UN Office of the High Commissioner for Human Rights) (2010). *Fact Sheet No. 34, The Right to Adequate Food*, April 2010, No. 34, https://www.refworld.org/docid/4ca460b02.html [accessed 30 March 2021]

Pearl, R., Meesters, H., Wanjiru, L., Dentler, A. and Meyreles, L. (2009). Training manual on gender and climate change. Aguilar, L. (Main Author) Module 4: Gender mainstreaming in adaptation efforts. International law instruments as a framework for mainstreaming gender in climate change. The International Union for Conservation of Nature (IUCN) and the United Nations Development Programme (UNDP) in partnership with the Gender and Water Alliance, ENERGIA International Network on Gender and Sustainable Energy, United Nations Educational, Scientific and Cultural Organization (UNESCO), Food and Agriculture Organization (FAO) and the Women's Environment and Development Organization (WEDO) as part of the Global Gender and Climate Alliance (GGCA).

Raney, T., Anríquez, G., Croppenstedt, A., Gerosa, S., Lowder, S. K., Matuschke, I., & Skoet, J. (2011). The role of women in agriculture. ESA Working Paper No. 11-02. Agricultural Development Economics Division, The Food and Agriculture Organization of the United Nations.

Rathgeber, E. (2009). Training manual on gender and climate change. Aguilar, L. (Main Author) Module 6: Gender-sensitive strategies on technology development and transfer to support actions on mitigation and adaptation. International law instruments as a framework for mainstreaming gender in climate change. The International Union for Conservation of Nature (IUCN) and the United Nations Development Programme (UNDP) in partnership with the Gender and Water Alliance, ENERGIA International Network on Gender and Sustainable Energy, United Nations Educational, Scientific and Cultural Organization (UNESCO), Food and Agriculture Organization (FAO) and the Women's Environment and Development Organization (WEDO) as part of the Global Gender and Climate Alliance (GGCA).

Schmidhuber, J., & Tubiello, F. N. (2007). Global food security under climate change. *Proceedings of the National Academy of Sciences*, 104(50), 19703-19708.

Siche, R. (2020). What is the impact of COVID-19 disease on agriculture?. *Scientia Agropecuaria*, *11*(1), 3-6.

Singh, S. P., Arya, M. P. S., & Srivastava, S. K. (2019). Gender Perspectives in Rice-based Production System in the Country. *RASSA Journal of Science for Society*, *1*(3), 142-148.

Umesha, S., Manukumar, H. M., & Chandrasekhar, B. (2018). Sustainable agriculture and food security. In *Biotechnology for Sustainable Agriculture* (pp. 67-92). Woodhead Publishing.

UNDP and GGCA. (2009). Resource guide on gender and climate change. URL: https://www.un.org/womenwatch/downloads/Resource_Guide_English_FINAL.pdf [accessed 21 April 2021]

UNEP DTU Partnership, UN Environmental, and GEF (2018). TNA (Technology Needs Assessment). https://tech-action.unepdtu.org/wp-content/uploads/sites/2/2019/07/web-tna-gender-guidebook-01.pdf [accessed 5 May 2021]

UNEP (United Nations Environment Programme) (2017). Training Module 3 Gender, climate change and food security, Senay Habtezion. https://www.undp.org/content/undp/en/home/librarypage/womens-empowerment/gender-and-climate-change.html [accessed 6 April 2021]

UNFPA and WEDO (Women's Environment & Development Organization and United Nations Population Fund) (2009). Climate Change Connections 5: Financing that Makes a Difference, 2009: https://www.unfpa.org/sites/default/files/pub-pdf/climateconnections_5_finance.pdf [accessed 29 April 2021]

UNESCO (2014). Priority gender equality action plan (2014-2021). https://unesdoc.unesco.org/ark:/48223/pf0000227222 [accessed 18 April 2021]

United Nations. Office of the Special Adviser on Gender Issues, & Advancement of Women, New York (2002). Gender mainstreaming: An overview. https://www.un.org/womenwatch/osagi/pdf/e65237.pdf [accessed 23 April 2021]

UN Women (2021). UN Women submission on "Gender-responsive mitigation and technology development and transfer" https://unfccc.int/files/documentation/submissions_from_non-party_stakeholders/application/pdf/503.pdf [accessed 10 May 2021]

Vermeulen, S. J., Aggarwal, P. K., Ainslie, A., Angelone, C., Campbell, B. M., Challinor, A. J., ... & Wollenberg, E. (2012). Options for support to agriculture and food security under climate change. *Environmental Science & Policy*, *15*(1), 136-144.

WBG, FAO & IFAD (World Bank Group, The Food and Agriculture Organization of the United Nations, & The International Fund for Agricultural Development) (2015). *Gender in climate-smart agriculture: module 18 for gender in agriculture sourcebook*.

Weiser, S. D., Young, S. L., Cohen, C. R., Kushel, M. B., Tsai, A. C., Tien, P. C., ... & Bangsberg, D. R. (2011). Conceptual framework for understanding the bidirectional links between food insecurity and HIV/AIDS. *The American journal of clinical nutrition*, 94(6), 1729S-1739S.

Williams, M. and Conze, Y. (2009). Training manual on gender and climate change. Aguilar, L. (Main Author) Module 7: Gender mainstreaming in climate change financing mechanisms. International law instruments as a framework for mainstreaming gender in climate change. The International Union for Conservation of Nature (IUCN) and the United Nations Development Programme (UNDP) in partnership with the Gender and Water Alliance, ENERGIA International Network on Gender and Sustainable Energy, United Nations Educational, Scientific and Cultural Organization (UNESCO), Food and Agriculture Organization (FAO) and the Women's Environment and Development Organization (WEDO) as part of the Global Gender and Climate Alliance (GGCA).

Ylipaa, J., Gabrielsson, S., & Jerneck, A. (2019). Climate change adaptation and gender inequality: insights from rural Vietnam. *Sustainability*, 11(10), 2805.

Zusman, E., Lee, S. Y., Rojas, A., & Adams, L. (2016). *Mainstreaming Gender into Climate Mitigation Activities: Guidelines for Policy Makers and Proposal Developers*. Asian Development Bank.

THE BICONDITIONALITY OF ART-POLITICS

*Barış ÇAĞLAR**

It is high time to correct the falsehood that art is a luxury. The fact of the matter is that art is actually a necessity without which politics are remarkably empoverished. It is all the more urgent to correct that falsehood in our current era owing to the pressures of globalization. Art is not distinct from life at large because art is life at our mirroring-minds. As such, it is not separate from politics. Both politics and art are about designing how we live. Figuring out problems and implementing response policies constitutes the most fundamental activities of that design. Both art and politics are the processes through which we humans shape life. Indeed, this is exactly the commonality where art and politics meet. However, the reason why politics all around the world has become lowly and insensitive to the demands of the citizens, and the reason why politics remains helplessly uncreative in solving local, national, regional and global problems is the contemporary absence of aesthetics in our societies.

Since aesthetics is a set of principles concerned with nature and appreciation of beauty, it transforms and feeds the human soul and mind so as to ameliorate the human condition. Yet, the reverse is also true: absence of aesthetics, especially in the activities of politicians, exacerbate the human condition even more. Thus, a feel for beauty of the living beings -plant, animal or human- comes from experiencing art. A feel and appreciation for beauty of animate beings brings about an enlightenment of human consciousness. Since art is

---

* Dr. Öğr. Üyesi, MEF Üniversitesi, İİSB Fakültesi, Siyaset Bilimi ve Uluslararası İlişkiler Bölümü, İstanbul, Türkiye, ORCID: 0000-0002-9294-3377.

about having or cultivating a culture for beauty, it is an endeavour that forms a particular mind-set and a breeze of soul that brings about anti-violence through acceptance, if not love. That is a mode of existence where one is socialized into learning and acquiring it in time by means of getting exposed to differents forms of beauty/artwork. Lofty as it may sound, it is not unrealistic though. Such a consistent exposure may inculcate individuals with keen eyes that see and appreciate the artful/beautiful in everything.

Such a social conditioning can only be realised via societal familiarity with and appreciation of art and the artful in every sector and moment of any job or occupation undertaken in daily happenstances. The glue and fabric of such social conditioning is exposure to anything and everything that is artful. 'Artful' means the acknowledgment and appreciation of the beauty of nature and all living beings. Anything artful or any artful touch, be it a lively and moving speech of a politician or a song, or a single flower on the street provides spiritual wherewithal for the laymen.

Appreciation of beauty in anything we experience is not only about intellect, but also morality and norms. It is about the right of others to exist independent of what we want them to do or not to do. Art, indirectly but nevertheless effectively, enlightens all voters and politicians alike by helping and encouraging them to question self-anointed or socially acceptedd extant outlooks on any issue-area. This originates from the inner working mechanism of art, which inculcates peaceful coexistence and respect for 'the other' whether that other is a tree, forest, an environmental problem or a group of people deemed hostile. Hence, art is not only about the intellect, but also about aesthetics, morality. and self-criticism. This is how art and artists bring forth ways and means to make us notice and grasp our basic motivations and self-engineered internal obstacles that in turn create political problems with 'others'. We not only come to see the othering process through which we demonize others, but also through art, we come to 'feel' what we do. That is exactly where artists are brilliant: in making us to remember that we are all human beings after all.

Art, much as politics does, creates a process through which we devise and design solutions to problems of othering. At each and every facet and sector of our everyday activities, art and politics coexist and they inter-are. Inter-are; that is, they cannot be separated from one another for artful humanism and the appreciation of peaceful coexistence with others is inevitable for the successful conduct of domestic and international politics. Unconscionable and cruel wars are the result of uncultivated minds that are restless even with the ideas of peace and cooperation. This is exactly why it is critically determinative for all nations and states to avoid living artless. The 21st century challenge for the whole peoples of the world is to resuscitate the will and beauty of living together without putting up a fight or war against one another. Artful politics and political art help achieve that.

The need to avoid living artless in any field, job or walk of life has become more apparent today especially when conventional or traditional categories have faded, intersected and sometimes disappeared altogether under globalization. The declining conceptual and narrative power of modernist terms that are binarily oppositonal do not help achieve peace between either gangs in streets or among groups in international fora. The distinction between art and politics is such a faint distiction in our day. Although this may sound contradictory in the first place, when looked closely, we observe that under-performance of one wears out the other. As this is the case, politics must be the art of solving our problems without resort to war. Anti-violence is the quintessential element that makes politics better. If we are to prefer dialogue and negotiation over warfare, law over chaos, morality or ethics over arbitrariness, then politics should be artful to achieve it. Politics can only become artful if and only if beauty of human life is appreciated in the conduct of politics. Concurrently, that would be a political process where ultra egotism is eliminated. Art (through the inculcation of the sanctity of human life) instills politicians, civil society and voters alike with a certain bit of pacifism/anti-violence and alturism.

That said, an embodiment might be provided with a real-world experience from the field: The public's contact with art and artists improves our ability to live a happier life. Devlet Tiyatroları Turneleri/the Turkish State Theaters Tours that travel to Anatolian cities during the second part of the 20th century Turkey were the glittering horizons for the common men and women at the behest of lesser developed inner lands of the country. As younger members of their families in which parents appreciate Lale Oraloglu and other precious artists with excitement, theaters constituted a different lane for the new generations to grow up along. The inseparable couple of art and politics, in enabling each other can also be refered to as 'art-politics', and much time has passed since Devlet Tiyatroları/Turkish State Theater campaigns toured and enriched the Anatolian heartland. Art-politics had a different time-space configuration back then. It is at a different stage now. In the intervening time, that is when we embark upon the beginnings of the 2000s, sociology and technology have changed. The Internet has deeply influenced the space where art and politics are made and financed. However, what is significant here is that art and politics have never really become completely separate from one another. Sometimes they nested inside each other and sometimes they, so to speak, erode and maim one another by biting and carving each other out.

The inseparable biconditionality of art-politics, which is often ignored in the 21st Century, urgently needs to be addressed because the modernist conception that art and politics are distinct does not correspond to our day. Such distinction purges politics of aesthetic feelings without which one cannot easily appreciate the beauty and sanctity of all humans' right to live. Put differently, artful politics or politics infused with the artful spirit of humanism makes room for peace-making. Thus, art-politics has a freedom dimension. Another dimension demostrates itself via rhetoric. Eloquence, skill, tact and lyrical addresses, enables sophisticated policies to be crafted and commnicated efffectively. When political discourses do not overlap the discourses of art, the art of speech is also lost - the effective expression and the anti-violence agenda go down together with it.

Still another and related dimension is technology-driven dynamics of time-space where art-politics is carried out. No matter how much we resist today's digital technologies, in a world where it is increasingly evolving into a cyber universe, a global digital culture has been created. This culture has also created a common language with images. As in many branches of art, theatre has been affected by this. To reiterate for the sake of emphasis and significance, the physical mobile Anatolian tours of Lale Oraloglu and his dear friends have been replaced today by virtual Anatolian touring. Politics and art can undoubtedly be considered and evaluated separately though. However, this is just an analytical distinction in our minds. The real world application on the ground does not see a separation between the two. The complementariness of the art and politics in reciprocally enabling themselves to exist in the very first place reminds us how important their coexistence has become. This is one of the manifestations of the postmodern practices of life. Art-politics reimagines and reproduces life each and every day. Art-politics starts each new day with a new production (discourse) and offers this production to consumption. This union has to carry out a new production every day due to globalization without repeating the previous one. If the inseparable union of art-politics is forced to work separately, it will quickly drawdown and exacerbate politics.

INDUSTRY 4.0 VISION TO REACH THE LEAN-SIX SIGMA TARGETS

*Mustafa BAYHAN**

Introduction

The industrialization movements that emerged in Western European countries in the 18th century and spread to the whole world from there, express the transition from agricultural economy to industrial economy and are called industrial revolutions. This process, which started with the use of steam, coal and iron, accelerated the production processes and achieved rapid development in mining and other industrial areas, especially in the weaving industry.

With this developing industrialization, the increase in production has increased the use of raw materials and energy. In this process, which developed with rapid industrialization, many waste started to occur and this led to an increase in costs. These developments have led to the emergence of the "Lean Manufacturing" philosophy, which aims to simplify the production and service processes in the enterprises and eliminate waste and thus reduce costs and increase customer satisfaction and ensure continuous improvement. Over time, it has become clear that just preventing waste in production processes is not enough. In addition, it will be possible to produce the right product in the right way by reducing the waste of faulty outputs with the improvements to be made in the production processes and quality control studies.

---

[*] Pamukkale University, Faculty of Economic and Administrative Sciences, Business Departmant, Denizli / TURKEY, ORCID: 0000-0001-5793-5390, mbayhan@pau.edu.tr.

1. Industrial Revalutions

In this chapter; The transformations and industrial revolutions in the industry, which started with the discovery of steam power and its use in machines, and continued with the discovery of electricity and the development of computer technologies, are discussed.

1.1. First Industrial Revolution (Industry 1.0)

The 1st Industrial Revolution is assumed to have started with the discovery of steam energy and its use in machines. Thomas Newcomen's steam-powered atmospheric engine (Figure 1), built in 1712, was the first practical reciprocating steam engine. Extremely inefficient by modern standards, this engine was used to power municipal water supply pumps, being used to dig deeper in mines, providing a major expansion in coal mining (Rolt and Allen, 1997).

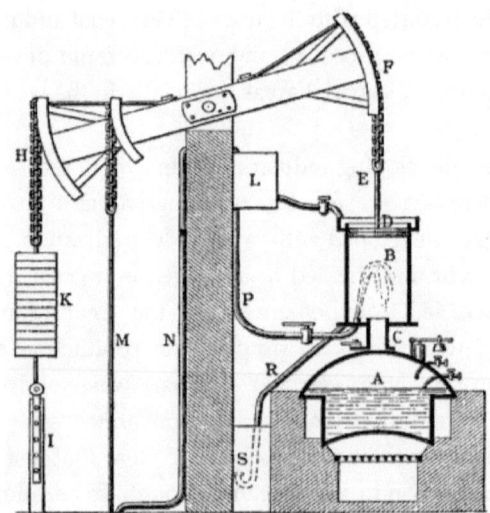

Figure 1. Newcomen's Steam-Powered Atmospheric Engine (Rolt and Allen, 1997).

In 1782, the industrial revolution gained functionality and was established in many mining enterprises in the UK in a short time when James Watt took the patent of the double-action rotary bottom steam machine (Figure 2) by developing Newcomen's machine in England. Watt's discovery of the steam engine was the driving force of the Industrial Revolution. This revolution took place at the end of the 18th century as a transition from agricultural economy to industrial economy. There has been a transition from hand and body labor to machine power in production. The steam engine invented by James Watt has rapidly developed in mining and other industries, especially in the weaving industry. After the invention of the steam engine, mechanization activities accelerated. Production has increased with mechanization, and intercontinental trade of the increased production has been possible with the spread of steam ships (Basalla,1996).

Figure 2. J.Watt's Steam Engine (1782)

The First Industrial Revolution, affecting the period between 1765-1850, started to show its effect with the mechanization of weaving looms in England. Along with this, as a result of the use of coal and steam instead of wood, the increase in the movement power has enabled mechanization and the transfer of production to factories, old model family companies and small workshops have been replaced by large factories (endustri40.com).

1.2. Second Industrial Revolution (Industry 2.0)

The second industrial revolution, which is considered to have started with the cheap steel production method invented by the British inventor Bessemer in 1860 and also called the "Technology Revolution", covers the years between 1850 and 1970 (Çeliktaş et al. 2015). The most important feature of this period is that mass production based on the division of labor in manufacturing with the use of electrical energy and mass production started with the establishment of assembly lines (Kagermann vd., 2013). The first example of this was the first assembly line slaughterhouses established in Cincinnati in 1870.

After the first industrial revolution started in England; Thanks to the expanding railway network, steel and cheap raw materials, electrical and chemical techniques, industrialization has improved and in a short time it has spread to countries such as Europe, America and Japan (Kabaklarlı,2016).

The technical advances that took place in the second half of the 19th century enabled electrical technologies to be used in production lines in factories for the first time, and this new technology contributed to the development of new production methods. The band type mass production style that Henry Ford developed for the first time in 1913 and applied in the automotive industry had a revolutionary effect (Figur 3). Based on mass production, low cost and standard product, this production model has been up-to-date for years and has been accepted as the 2nd Industrial Revolution (Alçın, 2016).

Figure 3. Fordist Production Form Automobile Assembly Line

In the second industrial revolution, steam power was completely used in industrial production and railways were built. These developments have made coal and iron as well as steel production increases the required. The mass production of steel and the realization of railways and the great contribution of electricity to production in factories have facilitated living spaces. In this period, the demand for energy resources in increasing industrial activities has changed from traditional steam power to energy resources based on oil and electricity (Kılıç and Alkan, 2018).

1.3. Third Industrial Revolution (Industry 3.0)

After the Second World War, a new industrial era was entered, especially with the use of electricity in mass production and the development of the production line. This period, named as the third industrial revolution, emerged with the use of programmable logic circuits (PLC), which caused the mechanical and electronic technologies to be replaced by digital technology in production. In 1969, the first programmable logic circuit (PLC), which is a microprocessor-based device that processes the information received from the sensors according to the program given to it and transfers it to the work staff, was developed by a group of engineers in Bedford, Massachusetts, and started a new era in the industry with the automation of production systems (Figure 4). With this development, the period that started in the 1970s and lasted until today was called the Third Industrial Revolution (Bosca, 2017).

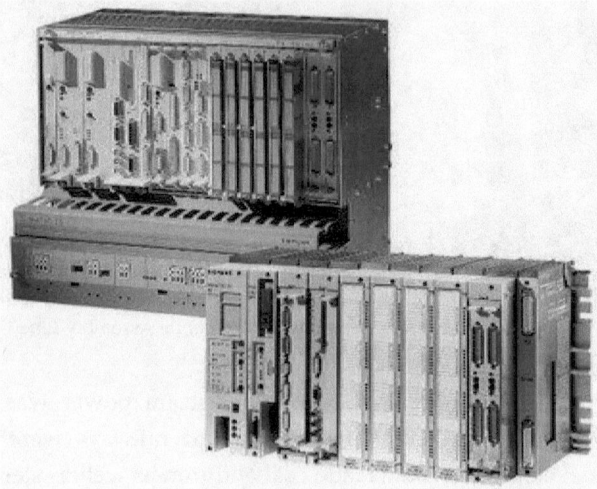

Figure 4. Allen Bradley - Modicon 084. First PLC (Csanyi,2011).

In this period, machines based on mechanical and electronic technology began to be replaced by digital technology-based machines in production. As a result of the developments in digital technologies, the rapid development of computers and the internet has spread the use of information processing and communication techniques and thus micro-electronic techniques, and the use of remotely controlled programmable machines in production has become widespread (Kılıç and Alkan, 2018).

1.4. Fourth Industrial Revolution (Industry 4.0)

This term, which first appeared at the Hannover Fair in 2011, is used to describe how this revolution will transform the convergence of global value chains. In 2012, the Industry 4.0 Working Group was formed. The project was described in detail with the final report prepared by this working group in 2013.

The First Industrial Revolution can be defined as the mechanization of production with the acquisition of steam power, The Second Industrial Revolution can be defined as the serialization of production with the use of electrical energy in the industry and the establishment of assembly lines, while the Third Industrial Revolution can be defined as the automation and digitization of production (Figure 5).

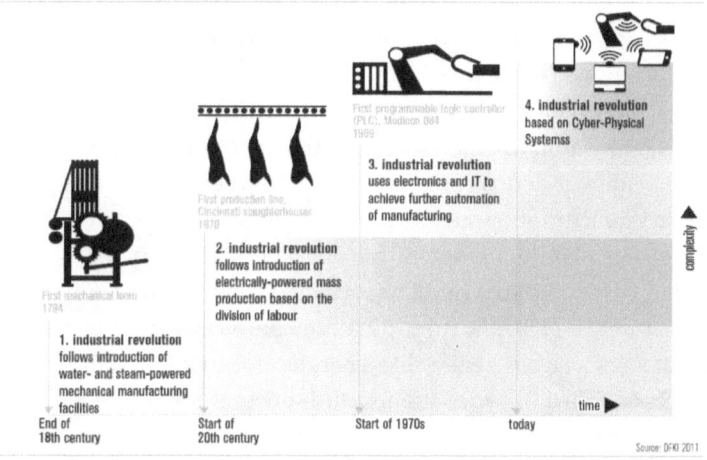

Figure 5. The four stages of the Industrial Revolution (Kagermann et al., 2013)

The new process, called Industry 4.0, includes a structure that will completely change the production and consumption relations. It defines the production systems that instantly adapt to the changing needs of the consumer on the one hand, and the automation systems that are in constant communication and coordination with each other on the other.

Mrugalska & Wyrwicka (2017) define the concept of industry 4.0 as "the integration of complex physical machines and devices with networked sensors and software used to better predict, control and plan commercial and social consequences" or "a new level of value chain organization and management throughout the life cycle of products".

Industry 4.0 is a collective set of technologies and concepts of value chain organizations. Based on the concept of cyber-physical systems, internet of things and services internet of. This structure contributes greatly to the vision of smart factories (endustri40.com). Industry 4.0 aims to enable objects to communicate with each other and with people by monitoring physical processes with cyber-physical systems in modular smart factories, and thus, to make decentralized decisions. The purpose of Industry 4.0 is not a factory that is dehumanized, but rather to create a human-oriented organization with high added value to all stakeholders with the use of information technology capabilities.

The fourth industrial revolution that made smart factories possible; Although it does not define a world where virtual and physical manufacturing systems cooperate flexibly with each other in the global plan, the scope of the concept of Industry 4.0 is much wider. In this context, simultaneous developments are taking place in a number of fields from quantum physics to high-end nanotechnologies, from renewable energies to quantum information processing. What makes the fourth industrial revolution different from its predecessors is the intertwining and fusion of these technologies and their mutual interaction in physical, digital and biological fields (Bosca, 2017).

1.4.1. Features of Industry 4.0

The basic idea of the fourth industrial revolution or Industry 4.0 as it is widely used, was put forward in Kagermann's article in 2011. In this study, Kagermann (2011) states that the fourth industrial revolution includes not only the development in automation, but also intelligent observation and decision-making processes. However, it is accepted that Industry 4.0 reached a theoretical framework, when the German National Academy of Science and Engineering (Acatech) published the subject as a "manifesto" in 2013.

In this report of Acatech, it is emphasized that Industry 4.0 will focus on the following overarching aspects (Kagermann et al., 2013):

- Horizontal integration through value networks

- End-to-end digital integration of engineering across the entire value chain
- Vertical integration and networked production systems
- Includes horizontal integration in value networks, smart cross-links within and between firms, and digitalization of value creation (Fig.6).

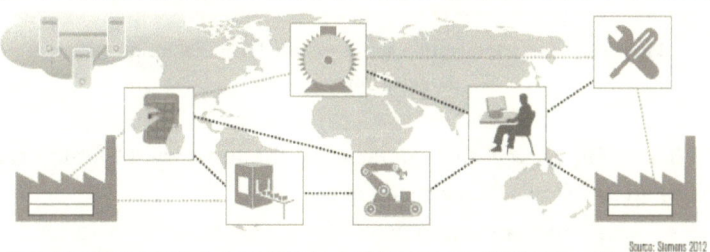

Figure 6. Horizontal integration through value networks
(Kagermann et al., 2013)

End-to-end engineering in the product life cycle includes smart cross-linking and digitalization at all stages of the product life cycle (service, production, production engineering, product design and development, production planning) (Fig. 7).

Figure 7. End-to-end engineering across the entire value chain
(Kagermann et al., 2013)

Connection and vertical integration in manufacturing systems; includes smart connectivity and digitalization at different levels of accumulation and hierarchical value creation in manufacturing lines, factories and production modules (Fig.8).

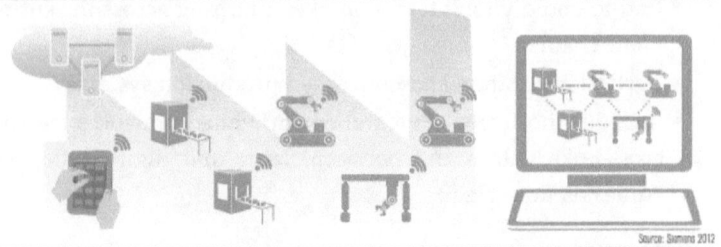

Figure 8. Vertical integration and networked manufacturing systems
(Kagermann et al., 2013)

The main aspects that characterize the Industry 4.0 vision can be listed as follows (Kagermann et al., 2013):
- As an important component of this vision, smart factories will be placed in inter-company value networks, characterized by end-to-end engineering that encompasses both the production process and the manufactured product, thereby it will link the digital and physical worlds.
- Smart products that can be uniquely identified in Industry 4.0 will know the details of their own production processes even while they are being made. This means they can semi-autonomously control the individual stages of their production of smart products in certain industries. At the same time, it will be possible to ensure that finished products know the parameters in which they can function optimally and can recognize signs of wear and tear throughout their life cycle. This information can be combined to optimize the smart factory in terms of logistics, distribution and maintenance and integration with business management applications.
- In the future, within the scope of Industry 4.0, it will be possible to include individual customer and product-specific features in the design, configuration, order, planning, production, operation and recycling stages. In this way, it will be possible to include last-minute change requests just before and even during production.

- Implementation of the Industry 4.0 vision; will enable employees to control, organize and configure smart production resource networks and production steps according to situation and context sensitive goals.

1.4.2. Components of Industry 4.0

There are numerous technologies and associated paradigms that make up Industry 4.0. These structures are called the components of Industry 4.0. Some of these components can be listed as (Fig.9):

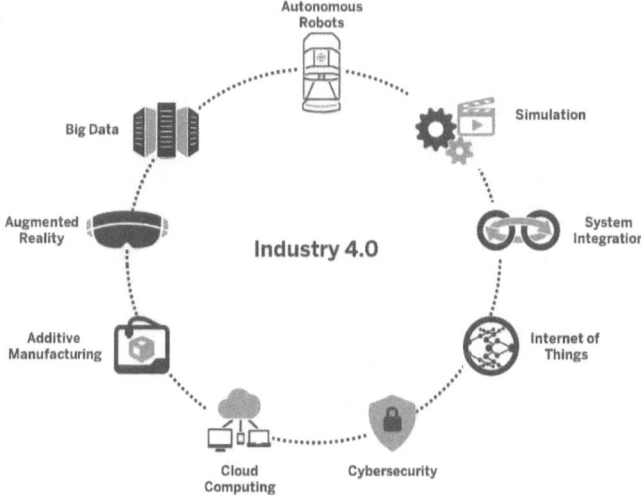

Figure 9. Industry 4.0 Components

- Cyber-Physical Systems- CPS
- Smart Factories
- Internet of Things-IoT
- Cloud Based Manufacturing-CBM (Kumar et al., 2019).

These features are not only highly associated with internet technologies and advanced algorithms, but also point out that Industry 4.0 is a value-added information processing and industrial value-added process.

Cyber-Physical Systems- CPS: The systems that connect the physical world and the cyber space with the internet are called cyber-physical systems. These systems connect the physical world with the virtual world with the help of sensors and actuators. Cyber-physical systems that unite these two worlds consist of two important elements. It consists of a network of objects and systems that communicate with each other via an internet address (internet of things) and a virtual environment that emerges by simulating real-world objects and behaviors in a computer environment (endustri40.com).

Smart Factories: In order to meet customer needs in the vision of Industry 4.0, a smart and dynamic manufacturing ecosystem is created within itself. In such an ecosystem, smart factories understand the state of the production process and react to a problem with minimal human intervention when a problem arises. If human intervention is required, the system collects and presents information in a way that leaves the least workload to the human (Suri vd, 2017).

The "smarter" of the factories refers to the factories that instantly respond to customer orders with less waste. The modern consumption structure is not only differentiated, but also changes instantaneously. Smart factories must be capable of enabling just-in-time production as well as diversified products (Kumar et al., 2019). With smart production in smart factories, thanks to the sensors, automation and perfected processes used in CPS, minimization of human factor and minimization of errors in the production process will be achieved.

Internet of Things-IoT: The Internet of Things concept, first used by Kopetz (2011), describes the ability to collect, reproduce and organize data from different sources in a workplace or factory. The Internet of Things offers a connectionless data management that speeds up process controls. This platform is effective in transforming big data into information that will activate the cyber-physical system (CPS). The Internet of Things (IoT) can be simply defined as a relationship between things (machines, products, places, etc.) and people made possible by connected technologies and various platforms (Schwab, 2016).

Cloud Based Manufacturing-CBM: Cloud computing technology, which forms the basis of cloud-based manufacturing, is a technology that enables the storage of big data on the internet and the accessibility of this data. With the development of cloud technology, the use of big data, which is one of the building blocks of Industry 4.0, has had the opportunity to be applied in the industry. The advantages of cloud computing include low hardware and software costs, ability to benefit from improved performance (access to the latest technology infrastructure continuously), ability to benefit from instant updates, high storage capacity provided, accessibility from different platforms and the suitability of this structure for group work (Tayaksi et al., 2016).

1.4.3. Goals of Industry 4.0

Industry 4.0; It is an approach that mainly aims at maximizing computerization in the manufacturing industry and therefore equipping production with high technology. In this way, it aims to achieve a higher level of automation with a higher level of operational efficiency and productivity (Lu, 2017). There are three main purposes here:

(1) Minimizing human labor in production and eliminating errors in production in this way.

(2) Providing the highest level of flexibility in production and thus obtaining the opportunity to make consumer-specific products.

(3) Speeding up production.

With Industry 4.0, it is aimed that physical parts, vehicles and machines communicate with each other over the internet, thus reducing the time in production and ensuring more efficient use of resources (Fortune, 2017).

It is possible to list the potentials of Industry 4.0 as follows (Kagermann et al., 2013):

Meeting individual customer needs: Industry 4.0 ensures that customer-specific criteria are included in the design, configuration, ordering, planning, production and operation phases, thereby enabling last minute changes.

Flexibility: Cyber physical system (CPS) based ad hoc networking; It provides dynamic configuration of different aspects of business processes such as quality, time, risk, durability, price and environmental friendliness. This makes it easier to constantly "organize" materials and supply chains. This also means that engineering processes can be made more agile, production processes can be changed, temporary shortcomings caused by supply problems can be compensated, and large increases in output can be achieved in a short time.

Optimized decision making: In order to be successful in a global market, being able to make the right decisions in a very short time is often a critical step. Industry 4.0 provides end-to-end transparency in real time, enabling early validation of engineering design decisions and both more flexible responses and global optimization across all facilities of a manufacturing company.

Resource productivity and efficiency: As comprehensive strategic objectives for industrial production processes, resource efficiency and resource efficiency also apply to Industry 4.0. Cyber physical systems (CPS) enable production processes to be optimized on a case-by-case basis across the entire value network.

Creating valuable opportunities through new services: Industry 4.0 opens up new ways to create value and new assignment forms across service channels. For this, valuable opportunities can be created by applying smart algorithms to large amounts of various data (big data) recorded by smart devices.

Responding to demographic change in the workplace: Interactive collaboration between people and technological systems will provide businesses with new ways to transform demographic change for their advantage.

Work life balance: More flexible business organization models of companies using cyber physical systems (CPS); means employees are well placed to meet their growing need for a better balance between their work and private lives, as well as personal and continuing professional development.

2. Lean Manufacturing And Six Sigma

In this section, the "Lean Manufacturing" philosophy, which was first put forward and implemented by the Japanese Toyota company under the leadership of Taiichi Ohno, and then the "Six Sigma" philosophy, also known as zero error, will be mentioned.

2.1. Philosophy of Lean Production

The basic principles of the lean production and management system were first laid in the Japanese Toyota company in the 1950s, under the leadership of engineer Eiji Toyoda, a member of the Toyoda family, and Taiichi Ohno, with whom he worked together. Today, the essence of the production method adopted by Toyota, which has spread to every country and all business lines, is simplicity. Lean Manufacturing, in its simplest form, is the reduction of the time from the production of the product to its distribution and delivery to the customer and the elimination of waste (Vincenti, 2002).

The starting point of the lean manufacturing system; It is simple thinking and the most important feature of the simple thought philosophy is to find and destroy where there is waste. Waste is at the center of lean manufacturing. Because, according to this philosophy, it is impossible to talk about leanness, lean thinking and lean production in an enterprise where there is waste (Yamak, 1998). The main purpose of this approach is to eliminate activities that do not add value (waste), to manage the entire production cycle on a value-based basis by making continuous improvements in processes and / or operations. In production facilities; The reduction of stock quantities, shortening of procurement, production and delivery times, ease of follow-up and control, rapid reduction of costs can be counted among the most important effects of lean applications (Can and Güneşlik, 2013).

The lean production philosophy that first emerged in Japan has attracted attention with the success of Japanese companies in the market and this philosophy has started to be applied in other countries, especially in America. Especially after the customs union agreement with the European Union (EU), companies in Turkey have also started to apply this philosophy. Enterprises, which have been operating in a rapidly changing and highly competitive market in recent years, adopt the lean production approach in order to improve their production processes. In doing so, they focus on small units and value streams to improve the quality, flexibility, and customer responsiveness of their production processes.

The main goal in a lean production system is to be able to perform the production process in the required amount and time, in a flawless and waste-free way. Lean production tries to find as many shortcuts as possible while reaching the result in the production of goods and services. Decreasing the number of transactions both decreases the cost, increases the speed and decreases the possibility of making mistakes. Every activity that does not produce added value in lean production is carefully researched and extracted from the system. In this way, both speed is gained and the workforce demand is reduced by reducing the workload (Fırat and Ceyhan, 2015).

2.2. Techniques of Lean Manufacturing

One of the most important goals of businesses to reduce waste, which they adopt; There are many techniques and tools it uses to implement the lean manufacturing approach. These techniques (Radhakrishan and Balasubramanian, 2008:

1) Kaizen
2) Six Sigma (6σ)
3) Five S (5S)
4) Total productive maintenance (TPM)
5) Cellular manufacturing
6) Just in time production
7) Pre-production planning (3P)
8) Lean enterprise supplier networks

In this study, "Six Sigma" technique, one of the most important techniques used in lean production, will be discussed.

2.3. Six Sigma (6 σ)

Six Sigma is a quality management philosophy aimed at high standards, and it is a method that predicts that as the number of sigma increases, changes will decrease according to the specified target. In this method, the performance of a firm in products and services is measured by sigma level. As we find the causes that cause deviation in business processes and make them harmless, the level of sigma will constantly increase. This means less errors in business and production processes. The goal in Six Sigma is to reach products and processes that will bring variability and deviation closer to zero and meet expectations perfectly. The Six Sigma Model provides benefits to companies in issues such as reduction in costs and error rate, efficiency, market share, increase in customer and employee satisfaction, and positive change in corporate culture. Six Sigma is an approach that has been proven over and over the world, which businesses must apply carefully in order to minimize defects and errors and achieve a quality level close to zero (3.4 per million defects or errors) (Atmaca and Girenes, 2009).

Six Sigma approach in the whole process from production to order taking; reveals the quality level of products, services and processes. This quality level, which is a numerical value, indicates how much there is deviation from zero error in the whole process. With Six Sigma, which allows the measurement of the quality level of processes, it can be seen numerically whether the processes are at the desired quality level and the value of the deviation, if any. In this way, key processes can be identified and corrective measures can be taken. The aim is to reach the Six Sigma quality level (Çabuk and Karayılmazlar, 2010).

2.3.1. Basic Principles of Six Sigma Approach

The important goal of the six sigma philosophy is to reduce errors as much as possible. For this, customers, processes and accompaniment should be emphasized. As a management system, the basic principles of Six Sigma are examined under six headings below (Tekin, 2008):

Customer Orientation: Customer orientation is the first priority in Six Sigma. Performance measurement in Six Sigma starts with the customer. It is defined by customer satisfaction and impact on all Six Sigma quality.

Data Based Management: The basis of the Six Sigma quality management system is to transform the data obtained as a result of quality improvement studies into information and to make the right decisions. As a result of the improvement studies, it is determined how many of the complaints have been eliminated and the progress in the improvement program is evaluated.

Proactive Management: The word "proactive" means taking precautions, taking action before it occurs in the Six Sigma management system. Thinking correctly before becoming Web applications, using the possible negativities correctly in advance in various aids.

Process Focus: In Six Sigma philosophy, the process is the place where the activity is and even the activity itself. Processes are the key to success in all areas such as company management, product and service design, performance measurement, increasing efficiency, and improving customer satisfaction.

Unlimited Cooperation: Unlimited cooperation in Six Sigma does not mean unconditional sacrifice. However, it requires an understanding of the real needs of end users and the relationships between processes. It also predicts the use of the information obtained from the relationship between the customer and the process in a way that will benefit all relevant persons and units.

Top-Down Education: It is the training of all stakeholders in the company, from the highest level manager to the lowest level employee, as in quality improvement studies.

2.4. Lean Six Sigma

Lean Six Sigma is a management approach formed as a result of the combination of two separate concepts, "Lean" and "Six Sigma" (Pepper ve Spedding, 2010). Its goal is to reduce the error rate to zero, to increase productivity, to perfect all business processes and to continuously increase customer satisfaction. The Lean Six Sigma method is not content with detecting and correcting errors, but is based on restructuring the business process in a way that does not make any mistakes from the very beginning. While Lean provides a feature that reduces inefficiency and waste at all stages of both production and service and increases speed, flexibility and quality, Six Sigma's data-oriented analysis provides precision and accuracy (Hilton and Sohal, 2012).

Table 1 shows the similar and different aspects of Six Sigma and Lean Manufacturing approaches. Six Sigma attaches great importance to reducing deviations. Deviation is a phenomenon that has a negative impact on customer satisfaction. Six Sigma is a customer-based management philosophy that focuses on process improvements that affect financial results. Strives to instill a culture across the enterprise by continually improving on problems and adopting data-driven decision making management to achieve better business performance. On the other hand, the primary driving force of Lean Manufacturing is to reduce waste. Lean Manufacturing focuses on identifying and eliminating the seven wastes involved in each process by using Just In Time (Jiang et al., 2004).

Table 1: Six Sigma and Lean Manufacturing Principles

Six Sigma Principles	Lean Manufacturing Principles
• Reducing deflection • Continuous improvement • Culture change • Data-driven management • Customer oriented • Earning-focused projects • Project-based organization • Focusing on financial results • Process improvement	• Identifying and eliminating the muda (seven wastes) • Producing products as much as demanded (JIT) • Understanding the customer • Continuous simplificiation of the product process • Minimum stock of goods, semi-finished products and raw materials • Optimizing the use of production resources

Ref.: Jiang et al., 2004.

Lean Six Sigma uses its strengths by combining the advantages of Lean Manufacturing and Six Sigma. Although both methods have their own strengths and weaknesses, better results can be obtained by using these two methods together.

2.5. Industry 4.0 and Lean Six Sigma

Taichii Ohno's Toyota Production System is based on two structures: Just in time production (JIT) and Autonomation (Jidoka) (Ohno, 1988). Autonomation is defined as "smart automation" where machines and operators have the authority to detect when an abnormal situation occurs and to stop the work immediately (Womack and Jones, 2012). Integrating both lean manufacturing areas and Industry 4.0 is an important area of research that needs to be explored extensively. With the use of cyber physical systems with Industry 4.0, it is thought that machines and devices in the factories of the future will operate autonomously without the need for human operators (Table 2). Such a scenario has revealed the concept of lean automation where robotic and automation technologies are used to achieve lean production. Therefore, automation in production has played an important role from the beginning of lean production and Industry 4.0 can be considered as progress in this field (Sanders et al. 2016).

Table 2: Use Cases to Integrate Lean Manufacturing with Industry 4.0

Industry 4.0	Lean Manufacturing	
	Principle: JIT	**Principle: Jidoka**
	Method: Kanban System	**Method: Andon**
Smart Operator	The employee receives information about the remaining cycle time with augmented reality.	Wearable computer systems retrieve malfunctions and show them to employees in real time.
Smart Product	Smart product contains information about Kanban to realize order-oriented production.	-
Smart Machine	Machines offer standard interface to receive and send Kanban.	Machines send malfunctions directly to smart operators and call other systems for troubleshooting.

Ref.: Kolberg and Zühlke, 2015.

The link between lean manufacturing and Industry 4.0 is discussed under three main headings:

Smart Product: Within the scope of continuous improvement processes, also called Kaizen in Japanese, smart products can collect process data for analysis during and after production. Also, a smart product can contain Kanban information to control production processes. An example of fully decentralized controlled manufacturing based on smart products, demonstrated by SmartFactoryKL at Hannover Messe 2014 in Germany. The presented work stations are produced autonomously according to the work schedule on the product. Although it is thrust-controlled production, the concept can be adopted for this order-oriented control system (Mrugalska and Wyrwicka, 2017).

Smart Machine: Technical facilities help employees avoid mistakes, according to Poka Yoke. With its computing capabilities and connectable sensors, CPS can be quickly and flexibly integrated in error-prone processes for support. SmartFactoryKL shows modular workstations based on standardized physical and information technology (IT) interfaces for several years; Installation time is less than ten minutes, based on the Single Small Scale Swap Interchange (SMED) principle (Kolberg, and Zühlke, 2015).

Smart Operator: In the Andon method, where employees must be notified as soon as possible in the event of a failure, the smart operator can shorten the time from failure to failure reporting. Equipped with suitable sensors, CPS recognizes faults and automatically triggers fault repair operations on other CPS. For example; a continuous stream of tracks is provided with augmented reality (AR) applications (Kolberg and Zühlke, 2015).

3. Conclusion and Evaluation

In this study, it is discussed how Lean Manufacturing - Six Sigma philosophy can be implemented by using the opportunities and resources provided by Industry 4.0. Thanks to integrated information and communication systems, the shortcomings of traditional practices can be overcome by increasing efficiency and eliminating waste. This shows that industries now have the benefits combined with real-time integration of the entire factory and also the assurance of zero waste generation. Six Sigma is generally defined as a production system that does not contain any unnecessary elements in its structure and in which elements such as error, cost, stock, labor, development process, production area, waste, customer dissatisfaction are minimized. Driven by modern information and communication technologies, Industry 4.0 is a standardized network approach where components and machines become intelligent and based on well-proven internet standards. In depth, it is seen that Six Sigma methods and Industry 4.0 technologies are intertwined with each other and trigger each other. In this context; The smart factories, internet of things, cloud-based manufacturing, big data, three-dimensional technologies, artificial intelligence, cyber-physical systems, wearable internet, blockchain and bitcoin components that we examined under the title of Industry 4.0 are intertwined in achieving the Six Sigma goal, which is the perfect quality goal, and seem to trigger each other.

The "smarter" of the factories refers to the factories that instantly respond to customer orders with less waste. The modern consumption structure is not only differentiated, but also changes instantaneously. Smart factories are planned in a way that will enable just-in-time production as well as diversified products. With the smart production in smart factories, and with advantages of the sensors, automation and perfected processes used in the CPS, minimization of human factor and minimization of errors in the production process will be achieved. In addition, it would be a more correct approach for enterprises to first improve their processes by applying Six Sigma methods and thus increase their productivity, and then to apply Industry 4.0 technologies to their systems that have been transparent, standardized and free from waste. In this way, integrating Industry 4.0 technologies into lean production methods will increase operating efficiency. Otherwise, using Industry 4.0 technologies in their systems without applying Six Sigma methods may delay getting the desired level of efficiency.

References

Alçın, S., 2016, Üretim için yeni bir izlek: Sanayi 4.0. Journal of life Eco-nomics, 3(2), 19 – 30.

Atmaca, E, Girenes, S.Ş. 2009. Literatür Araştırması: Altı Sigma Metodolojisi, Süleyman Demirel Üniversitesi İktisadi ve İdari Bilimler Fakültesi Dergisi, 14(3), 111-126.

Autonomation (Jidoka), https://www.leansixsigmadefinition.com/ Available at: 20.05.2021.

Basalla, G. 1996. Teknolojinin Evrimi, Çev. C. Soydemir, Tübitak, Ankara.
Bosca, N. 2017. Endüstri 4.0: Bugüne Kadar Geçen Süreç, Nazmi Bosca Web Sitesi: https://nazmibosca.com/2017/01/29/endustri-4-0-bugune-kadar-gecen-surec/ Available at: 11.10.2020.
Can, A.V, Güneşlik, M. 2013. Yalın Yönetim Felsefesinin Önemli Bir Boyutu Olarak Muhasebede Yalınlaşma Düşüncesi ve Bir Yalın Muhasebe Uygulaması Örneği: Kendine Faturalama, Muhasebe ve Finansman Dergisi, 57, 1-22.
Csanyi, E., 2011. Industrial Automation; When we started to use PLCs after all? https://electrical-engineering-portal.com/when-we-started-to-use-plcs-after-all , Available at: 20.05.2021.
Çabuk, Y, Karayılmazlar, S. 2010. Altı Sigma Yaklaşımı, Journal Of Bartin Faculty Of Forestry, 12(17), 93-99.
Çeliktaş, M.S, Sonlu, G, Özgel, S, Atalay, Y. 2015. Endüstriyel Devrimin Son Sürümünde Mühendisliğin Yol Haritası, Mühendis ve Makina, 56(662), 24-34.
https://www.endustri40.com/ Available at: 15.09.2020.
Fırat, İ, Ceyhan, S., 2015. Yalın Üretim Sistemine Geçişin İşletme Performansına Olan Katkısı Kahramanmaraş'ta Hazır Giyim İşletmesinde Bir Uygulama Çalışması Örneği, Bingöl Üniversitesi Sosyal Bilimler Enstitüsü Dergisi, Yıl: 5/ Cilt: 5/ Sayı:9/ Bahar 2015.
Fortune Turkey, 2017. Akıllı üretim çağı: Endüstri 4.0, https://www.fortuneturkey.com/akilli-uretim-cagi-endustri-40-42841 Available at: 16.09.2020.
Hilton, R.J, Sohal, A. 2012. A Conceptual Model For The Successful Deployment Of Lean Six Sigma, International Journal Of Quality and Reliability Management, 29(1), 54-70.
Jiang, J. C., Chen, K. H., Wu, M. C. 2004. Integration of Six Sigma and Lean Production, In 33rd International Conference on Computers and Industrial Engineering.
Kabaklarlı, E. 2016. Endüstri 4.0 ve Paylaşım Ekonomisi, Dünya ve Türkiye Ekonomisi İçin Fırsatlar, Etkiler ve Tehditler, Nobel Yayınevi, Ankara.
Kagermann, H, Wahlster, W, Helbig, J. 2013. Acatech: Recommendations for Implementing the Strategic Initiative Industrie 4.0, Final Report of the Industry 4.0 Working Group.
Kılıç, S, Alkan, R.M. 2018. Dördüncü Sanayi Devrimi Endüstri 4.0: Dünya ve Türkiye Değerlendirmeleri, Girişimcilik İnovasyon ve Pazarlama Araştırmaları Dergisi, 2(3):29-49.
Kolberg, D, Zühlke, D. 2015. Lean Automation Enabled By Industry 4.0 Technologies. Ifac-Papersonline, 48(3), 1870-1875
Kopetz H. 2011. Internet of Things. In: Real-Time Systems. Real-Time Systems Series. Springer, Boston, MA. https://doi.org/10.1007/978 1 4419 8237 7_13.
Kumar K., Zindani D., Davim J.P. 2019. Intelligent Manufacturing. In: Industry 4.0. SpringerBriefs in Applied Sciences and Technology. Springer, Singapore. https://doi.org/10.1007/978-981-13-8165-2_1.

Lu, Y. 2017. Industry 4.0: A survey on technologies, applications and open research issues, Journal of Industrial Information Integration, Volume 6, Pages 1-10, https://doi.org/10.1016/j.jii.2017.04.005.

Mrugalska, B, Wyrwicka, M. K. 2017. Towards Lean Production in Industry 4.0, Procedia Engineering, 182, 466-473.

Ohno, T. 1988. Toyota Production System: Beyond Large-Scale Production. Cambridge, Mass.: Productivity Press.

Pepper, M.P.J., Speddıng, T.A. 2010. The Evolution of Lean Six Sigma, International Journal Of Quality and Reliability Management, 27(2), 138-155.

Radhakrishan, R, Balasubramanian, S. 2008. Business Process Reegineering - Text & Cases, New Delhi: PHI Learning Pvt.

Rolt, L.T.C., Allen, J.S. 1997. The Steam Engine of Thomas Newcomen, Landmark Publishing, Ashbourne.

Sanders, A., Elangeswaran, C., Wulfsberg, J. P. 2016. Industry 4.0 implies lean manufacturing: Research activities in industry 4.0 function as enablers for lean manufacturing. Journal of Industrial Engineering and Management (JIEM), 9(3), 811-833.

Schwab, K. 2016. Dördüncü Sanayi Devrimi, Optimist Yayınları, İstanbul.

Segovia, V. R. and Theorin, A. 2012, History of Control History of PLC and DCS. University of Lund.

Suri, K, Cuccuru, A, Cadavid, J, Gerard, S, Gaaloul W, Tata, S. 2017. "Model-Based development of modular complex systems for accomplishing system integration for Industry 4.0", 5th International Conference on Model-Driven Engineering and Software Development (MODELSWARD 2017), Feb. 2017, Porto, Portugal.

Taş, H.Y., 2018. Dördüncü Sanayi Devrimi'nin (Endüstri 4.0) Çalışma Hayatına ve İstihdama Muhtemel Etkileri, Uluslararası Toplum Araştırmaları Dergisi,9(16), 1817-1836.

Tayaksi, C., Ada, E, Kazancıoğlu, Y., 2016. Bulut Üretim: İşlemler Yönetiminde Yeni Bir Bulut Bilişim Modeli, Ege Akademik Bakış, C.16, Özel Sayı, 71-84.

Tekin, M. 2008. Altı Sigma, Günay Ofset, Konya.

Vincenti, A., 2002. Lean Machine, Automotive Engineer, 27(1), 58-59.

Womack, J.P, Jones, D.T. 2012. Yalın Düşünce, Optimist Yayınları, İstanbul.

Yamak, O. 1998. Kalite Odaklı Yönetim, Sinerji Yayınları, İstanbul.

Yıldız, A. 2018. Endüstri 4.0 ve Akıllı Fabrikalar, Sakarya University Journal of Science, 22 (2), 546-556.

THE COUNTER HEGEMONY AREA Of PAST EXTENDED TO PRESENT ON THE AXIS OF THE MEMORY: DOCUMENTARY FILM

Seher SEYLAN

Introduction

The cinema, paved the way by the Lumiere brothers, reflected daily and ordinary events on the screen in its early years. With the thematic films shot by George Melies, it has been revealed that the cinema can tell a story. The events that make up a story in these films take place in a certain time and the form chosen while the events are told affects the time organization of the film. The director, if wishes, carries the present to the past and the past to the present with this opportunity provided by the language of cinema (Hakan, 2011: 67). In other words, for the first time in its history with cinema, humanity can turn back and freeze the time.

Cinema takes us to the past in memory. The past leaves traces on the person, thus enabling him to gain various experiences. Cinema conveys these experiences, emerging today and carried into the future, to the audience. On the other hand, cinema reproduces time through time. Cinema, as an institution that provides usable images especially for mass consumption, has long been aware of its ability to produce experiences and upload memories to them, and these memories turn into experiences in which the audience is captivated and creates a change of emotion (Landsberg, 1995: 176). The memories collected by the past and carried to the present bear the traces of the human being and the society in in which exists. Cinema, plays a key role in revealing these traces is the answer for those who seek artistic answers to questions about the past of human and sociality, which affects our mental activities in establishing a connection between the present and the past (Makal, 2014: 13). This relationship with the past is sometimes the social past, great victories, lost wars, sometimes personal histories, struggle, and defeats. According to Jean Claude Carrier, who thinks that almost every period of history in cinema is researched and processed, cinema reveals the past. It recreates fabrics, clothes, people's gestures, languages. So, it can take the Vikings to Africa and the Martians to Babylon. For example, Maciste, the legendary hero of the Italians, fought Hercules on the motion picture screen. We do not know where or when the incident took place. In the movie in question, there is a cruel sultan, tortured slaves, a half-naked woman, monsters, white horses, revelers, wars, firearms. However, as the cinema recreates the before mentioned past, it organizes venues, period clothes, fake battles, extras that enacted armies with thousands of soldiers, horses, camels, lions, elephants, carriages and weapons, these moving images break the rings of the learning processand interrupt the ability to understand and evaluate the past (Makal as cited Coolingwood and Carter: 15-16).

It is the documentary about the real places instead of created spaces, people from life instead of fugurans, and experiences instead of stories. Although reality is a phenomenon that is not directly under the monopoly of documentary cinema, constitutes the main starting point and even existence point of the documentary cinema. Documentaries tell real stories about real people in real places. The themes have turned into struggles for the existence of ordinary people, those left on the sidelines, the forgotten, rather than the great events of great people (Aytekin, 2018: 48). The documentary is a means of bringing the long forgotten, ignored, and perhaps unnoticed lives of the past to the present.

Recently, the issues that documentary films handled in Turkish cinema has become a platform to express themselves those marginalized. Director Serdar Onal tells the story of Derdo Yıldırım, had to migrate from Kumk village of the Mutki district of Bitlis to

Istanbul in the documentary *Mother Derdo and the Walnut Tree*[1]. As we have seen in most of today's documentaries, the director questions the hegemonic ideology in the documentary *Mother Derdo and Walnut Tree* in the face of concrete historical and social events. In this study, *Mother Derdo and the Walnut Tree* (Onal, 2017) was awarded the "Best Documentary" at the 2017 Istanbul Film Festival, with the feature of the documentary to turn into a field of counter-hegemony for invisible identities and the journey of the past expressed in this counter-hegemony process, will be analyzed with Bergson's Matter and Memory approach.

In the study, firstly, the process of remembering the past and carrying it to the present will be examined with examples from the documentary on the axis of the Matter and Memory Approach[2]. It will be mentioned how the past is remembered to express it today, and then the counter-hegemony role of the documentary will be explained at the point of expressing the remembered past.

Remembering: From the Unmoving Past to the Moving Present

Bergson, the first thinker evaluated the cinematic mechanism as moving matter and discussed it extensively, is regarded as the first theorist of cinema. Concepts that Bergson brought to cinema are movement, travel, time, past, present, experiences and image (Sofuoğlu, 2004: 1). These concepts brought to cinema by Bergson explain how cinema connects the past and the present. The writer uses the pen to tell the past, and the director who wants to tell the past uses the camera instead of the pen. A trip to the past is taken with the camera. As a person goes on a spatial journey, also travels

---

[1] Derdo, an Armenian woman from Bitlis, migrated to Istanbul with her 8 children after the death of her husband in a land fight in 1975 and established a new life in Istanbul. She goes to her village in Bitlis every year, stays there for a while, collects her walnuts, and returns to the big city. The walnut tree is like a reflection of Derdo with its upright posture and the memory, it preserves (https://www.tsa.org.tr/tr/film/filmgoster/8668/derdo-ana-ve-ceviz-agaci).

[2] In this study, Hengri Bergson's Matter and Memory theory was used. For this reason, only the books written on the subject was taken as a reference and Bergson's views on this subject were included.

mnemonic. According to Butor, the present in this narrative, tells about the journey from the past to the present, should be a time that often breaks in the past and changes the essence and color of the past. Although the past has long been behind in time, the person relives that moment every time when returns to the past in his/her memory. The past is always there in the present to be remembered and experienced again. In other words, the past and the future of a person is a void that is still waiting to be filled in the present by the person's action (Hakan, 2011: 68). Derdo wants to fill this gap by returning to her village and spending time with her two Armenian friends. At the opening of the documentary audience witness, to the village of Derdo; her going to the land where she was born, raised, married, had children, and had to leave.

The village, where the past has inflicted deep wounds on her, is also the place she returns to heal her wounds. On this journey or every time, she arrives in her village, Derdo embarks on a journey into her past. This time, the audience also accompanies her memory journey. During the time spent in the village with Derdo, audiences witness what she remembers about her past, how she lost her husband, why she had to leave the village, how she migrated to Istanbul, and more so, her childhood memories.

Remembering something is actually remembering yourself. Many experiences such as what routes a person has passed during his/her life, who he /she is with and what has experienced means that he/she remembers himself/herself in the "now". The place where all these experiences are stored is memory. Memory helps us to keep past events by keeping information about the past in mind (Boyer and Wertsch, 2011: 5). The past does not disappear, it continues to exist in memory as the memory carries something from the past to the moment.

According to Bergson's Matter and Memory Theory, things remembered live in memory and thus interfere with things in the present. Past and future are not mutually external. Both are mixed in the unity of consciousness. However, the past that continues its eternal existence in memory is no longer movable, "now" it is moving (Çelikaslan, as cited in Russell, 2016: 3). On the other hand, there is no mechanical consciousness that records the past as it is. Events have impressions, effects, and remembrance of them. In Ancient Greece, two separate words were used for the verb to remember, "mneme" and "anamnesis", the first of which is the "memory" that appears passively, in the same words, which appears suddenly. Just as a feeling comes to mind, a pathos. The second one is the "memory" that comes out as a result of a search called recall in mind, rather than being passive. From this point of view, we can say that to remember is to pursue a memory and search for that memory. In this quest, the memory often comes back in imagination. It is seen that the presence constituting the representation of the past is the presence of an image. With this image, which can be audio-visual, abstract, or concrete, a past event is easily visualized in our minds (Ricoeur, 2011: 22-24). On the other hand, to dream is not to remember. As long as a memory takes place in the memory, it tends to live in an image, of course, but the opposite is not true, and in order for the direct image to take the person to the past, it must really go to the past to seek it and thus follow the continuous progress that takes the past from darkness to light (Bergson, 2015: 102-103).

The past is often moved by matter, which is a reminder of memories. Thus, experiences are reimagined in the mind. In other words, the past is re-imagined in the mind with this item (Bergson, 1998: 11). The image-matter that moves the past in the documentary is the walnut tree. Walnut resurrects past life and reminds us of past pain. By witnessing all the bad memories of the past, Derdo never wants to sell the walnut tree that reminds us of those days today. He states that he does not give up on the lands of her past with the walnut tree,[3] which she explains, "*I do not sell, it is there, like a bride, to the grave, looks to the village, to the house.*"

---

[3] At the opening of the documentary, we see the Kamk village of Bitlis after a long way. A walnut tree rooted in the ground welcomes us. Wherever she migrated, Derdo's roots are here. Derdo who comes to the village every summer, spends time with her two remaining Armenian friends. The fact

It is almost like a tree saying that its roots are there. In other words, the reason why she did not give up the walnut tree is that the walnut is the object that connects it to the past and present. The walnut tree, which has witnessed her experiences and contains Derdo's past like layers of memory, activates and reminds the past. The most important motive mechanism for remembering the past in the documentary is the walnut tree, and when the walnut tree enters the frame, we witness Derdo remembering and sharing the past. *"My father lived without food and water, grew up, worked hard, bought a field, looked after it, made money. There was a silver cube. His stepmother said, "son come hide it, they will come and get from us". He sees that he is hiding under the walnut tree next door. Her mother says, "nobody saw you, right?" "No, no" says "there was only one woman cooking across the street, she saw it"" that's enough" her mother says, but her mother was foolish, go and get it. They didn't not go in the morning. They said to the woman, if you took it, half of you would be ours. The woman sweared I didn't take it.... The woman had five sons ... Then one day her son came to my father, "Uncle, halal your right. I will go to the military and I will not come". Dad, why are you saying that son, God forbid, does that happen? " said." No," said the child, "my mother took your money, she swore on us". He did not return from the soldier. What can I say? They say we can eat the right of this nation and be full, they become worse. "*

On the other hand, in this case, the memory's use of past experience for present action, in other words, recognition must occur in two ways. Recognition is sometimes involved in the action, and the appropriate mechanism is fully automatic; however, sometimes it requires a memory study and the memory attempts to search the past to find the designs most likely to be involved in the situation and direct them to the present (Bergson, 2015: 59). Derdo and her children recall the difficulties they faced when emigrating from the

---

that Derdo goes to the village every summer despite all the experiences and all the pain is a desire to protect her land, in other words, her past, even if it has no financial value. The bond with the land is actually the bond with the past. It means I'm here (Onal, Face-to-Face Interview,2020).

village after their father was murdered:*"This was small in my arms, and the others had a very large stream on my skirts, the children passed, I was very afraid that the water will go away"* ... *"We did not come to Istanbul in a normal way, there was nothing to do, they (the villagers) required us to leave. They took us and we came to church, we stayed in the church for 2 or 3 months. There was no place there...Then we rented a house in Gedikpasha, although we didn't have anything nice to tell, you know the old houses, like a lunch box, we were staying in a room for 12 people, there was not enough room to sleep, we slept upside down, there was no space left for me There was a walk-in closet, I would lie bent over it. Maybe that is why my diseases have always happened"*.

This experience, which they shared with them and left deep traces in their lives, was once again remembered collectively; the conversation ended in a deep silence with sighs. The experience that the memories collectively remember shows its spiritual weight on the faces of each.

According to Russell, each mental state reflects the entire personality. Although each emotion is simple, it carries the entire past and present of the being that experiences it. The past that is no longer moving, still comes to light again in the present. The past is just a thought, now the giant against this thought is the action. Throughout the documentary, we see this movement as an act of remembering and sharing (Çelikaslan as cited in Russell: 3). Derdo does not just remember and tell her past experiences. While visiting her lands and vineyards, she is in present, telling that the places planted and planted in the past remained dry, even if they wanted to sell these lands, the villagers said *"The places are ours, the Armenians have nothing"* and even if the land is not cultivated, she is now opening the waterways. In memory, the past, the future, and the present are experienced simultaneously. However, in the same way, it can be likened to the continuous wrapping of a ball. Because our past follows us, the present that it collects along the way it follows, constantly rising to the present. The place where the past and the future live now is memory. The past does not appear as a thought in our mind, it is in the present, in the present (Bergson, 1998: 11).

In other words, memory is the preservation and accumulation of the past in the present: whether it now clearly carries the ever-growing image of the past, or it witnesses the burden that we drag behind us, with its constant change of character, the burden that gets heavier as we age, the past has not ceased to exist. With its uselessness and its distance from action, its inaccessibility, it still exists. The past coincides with being. We cannot say that the past exists because it is the state of being. It is the way of being hidden. It should be said that the present has already existed at any moment, the past exists, and has always existed before and after (Bergson, 1998: 11). In other words, the past is beside us with the state of being remembered, rather than being lived and finished.

Everything we remember about the past, whether happy or sad, is recorded in our memory as memory. While the memory keeps the "what, when, where" information about an event, it is based on the imaginary revisiting of the scene of the event experienced (Boyer and Wertsch: 7-8). While we are looking for a memory that we cannot think of, we are aware that we are already detaching ourselves from the present and looking for a past-finished event in which we first settle in the past in general and then in a certain area of the past. We engage in the search by a manual procedure like a camera set up. But our memory is still alive. Thus, we are prepared to remember the memory by taking an appropriate attitude. The memory appears gradually like a cloud layer that is densifying, then regains its past state from its vivid state (Boyer and Wertsch: 96). In the conversations of Derdo with her relatives and her friends Habibe and her sister, pain and happiness are together. Habibe and Derdo, who welcomed the shooting team with a smile and joy, talk about what they will offer to the guests. Derdo told Habibe about where she took the shooting crew around. Habibe *"did they see the cemetery?"* she asks and gives a deep sigh. After silence for a while, a sad conversation begins. Habibe said, *"Those were the days, so many men, women, so many gone, where did so many crowds go. Only you and me and my sister remain". Do they know that our husbands are dead?"* she asks. "I did not tell," says Derdo and adds; *"We are like strangers in our own home". "If I had a husband, I would have hosted my guests now."*

After this sad scene, we see that these three Armenian women who stayed in the village chat with pleasure. They joke and laugh at each other about which one is older. They feel very pleasant and happy. Then, when it comes to the grave again, a deep silence and sadness fall into the scene. So, in the next scene we see these three women at the head of their husbands' graves. They pray, weeping in sadness. Remembering is not just a remembrance of past actions and experiences, but also a re-experiencing of the emotional content of a past event. Throughout the documentary, when these three women, who are sometimes sad, sometimes laughing, sometimes sing, remember the past, we see the emotional traces of what happened and what they feel today. It is settled in the human soul as the experiences gained over time (Tarkovski, 1986: 62). One of the things that connect these three women here is the graves of their husbands, which carry their past to the present. For Bergson, who claims that everything is in an uninterrupted change, the present moment itself is changing. Their happy mood, laughing and having fun while having breakfast, changes to the grave. During a fun conversation, their mood turns from happiness to sadness with a word that suddenly turns them back into the past. Thus, as here, memory carries things from the past to the present and continues to exist.

While trying to remember, we first settle in the past in general and then in a specific area of the past (Deleuze, 2005: 91-101). The functioning of memory is like that of language. The way we understand what we are told is the same as the way we find a memory. We do not form the meaning from the sounds heard and the combined images; We settle first on the meaning layer and then on a certain part of this layer. No matter what now is involved, you can never recreate the past with the present; Image alone can only take me back to the past if I have already started looking for it in the past. We see the effect of taking matter, object, or image into the past in the walnut tree and walnut tree and in the walnut product.

Derdo remembers the past in general and later her father's memory about the walnut tree. While chatting with Hasan, the only person who helped her after losing her husband, although she lost her husband along time ago, remembers all the details. According to Bergson, memory also grows forever and "increases more and more like an endless burden, memories are never forgotten, they are simply stored and subject to perception and recall. Memory is always frugal, so nothing is "lost" (Bergson, 1998: 21).

According to Onal, difficulties were so embedded in Derdo's memory that she did not forget anything she experienced, on the contrary, she remembered everything word by word. She shared everythings could not tell or express in the past to Onal in details (Onal, 2020). The point of intersection between memory and matter is the moment. The matter that moves the memory carries the memory to the present, remembering memory tends to share. People tend to share memories of their past, even though they do not stimulate any emotion. On the other hand, when a past event is remembered, strong emotions are triggered by itself, the tendency to share is higher. Classical studies in the community psychology literature have shown that when people experience strong emotions (which are often negative emotions from stress), they tend to get closer to other people. This is actually a part of the effort to express the feelings within (in Ricoer's book, Lambert et al., 2011: 258). A person only opens himself and his past to those she finds close.

Throughout the documentary, the warm relationship between Derdo, Habibe and the director draws attention. Habibe calls the director "*my son*". The warm friendship between the three of them before the documentary continues after the shootings. This tight bond and intimacy between them enable Derdo and her relatives to comfortably talk about the past. So where are relatives in memory? According to Ricoeur, bonds with relatives include lineage and kinship relations, on the other hand, social relations dispersed according to various forms of belonging or reciprocal orders, these relationships can sometimes be formed by marriage bond. On the other hand, how do we take relatives into this account in terms of shared memory? Being together with relatives gives a special sound to life. The tone in question is related to two events that limit human life, namely birth and death. By the way, our relatives are those who confirm our existence in the same way that we accept their existence. What we expect from our relatives is that they will confirm our testimony. It is our ability to take responsibility for our actions, our ability to speak, to be able to act and to express (Ricoeur: 152).

Derdo says that she will ask Habibe for help if something happens, she will not ask anyone else. This connection established with experiences is so strong that Habibe states that if Habibe does not go to the village, Derdo will not go. Onal says that there are important places in the life of Derdo in three different geographies, namely Kumk Village, Istanbul, and Yerevan, where the documentary was shot, because in these places Derdo had acquaintances and relatives (Onal, 2020). There are Habibe and her older sister in Kumk village, her children and grandchildren in Istanbul, and her son, daughter-in-law and grandchildren in Yerevan and acquaintances whom she could only meet after the border was opened in the 90s. The acquaintances are the ones who both share the common pain and listen to the story with all ears. For example, one of the most important common points that hold these three women together in the village are the graves. Their wives sleep in a small Armenian cemetery, where they also have relatives. According to Önal, the graveyard of these women also has a great impact on their desire to be there (Onal, 2020).

In these 3 geographies, there are relatives who will listen to what Derdo says and share her pain and sorrow. On the other hand, she takes those who confiscated their property and home after losing their spouse to court. In that process, Mr. Hasan, who worked in the courthouse, was the only one who helped him. In the documentary, Derdo and Mr. Hasan get together again and talk about the old days. Hasan explains how Derdo struggled. However, during the conversation, a phone call comes from Sabri,

Derdo's son in Yerevan. While Hasan was addressing Sabri and asking laughingly *"Is there a map?"*. This scene shows that those with common pains remember the past in a similar way and understand each other much better. On the other hand, although those who witness the difficulties experienced do not have bad intentions, their current situation and, accordingly, their evaluation of the future differ.

Human memory carries the past to the present, so that the past can exist in memory at any moment. On the other hand, if we consider that memory has two ends, one end of it is directed towards the past, expanded in the past and the other is squeezed towards the future. Derdo says that everything was wasted while wandering around the fields, and maybe she thinks that these uncultivated lands will not leave traces of her family in time. Still, Derdo continues his struggle for the future, while telling the past on the one hand, and opening a waterway on the other. The waterway she opened shows that she did not lose hope despite everything, she did not give up on those lands. In another scene, we see Derdo breaking the walnuts she took to Istanbul for her grandson. Derdo, who does not leave the village without walnuts, establishes the bonds of future generations with the past with walnuts and wants this bond not to be broken. The past must be carried into the future. On the other hand, the past and the matter that takes me to the past enables the basic puzzle that we call the present representation of something past (Riceour, 2012: 473). Onal explains the relationship between the walnut tree, which Derdo does not return to Istanbul without collecting walnuts every year, and Derdo as follows; The walnut tree is an old tree that has witnessed everything that happened there. Right next to Derdo's house. Derdo waits for the walnuts to come to Istanbul. Because she wants to carry something from his generation to Istanbul, to her grandchildren. This is like a bond, like the desire to keep the bond between generations and not to break from its roots... She remembers the past by looking at the walnut tree (Onal, 2020). Just like Derdo's memory, the walnut tree witnessed everything that happened.

In addition to these images, places that give reference to the past and the future stand out in the documentary. Places that have changed throughout the documentary are Kumk village, Istanbul and Yerevan. The village tells us more about the past, while in Istanbul and Yerevan we feel ourselves in the present, but when it comes to the past in both places, it turns to the past in a memory journey. The future of Derdo's children is in Istanbul and Yerevan. They don't want to go to the village. Onal attributes this reluctance to their reluctance to go back to a past where their father was killed (Onal, 2020). On the other hand, Derdo does not want to leave her house. Because the mind that is not in the present is either in the past or in the future. While Derdo lives in the present with her past, she wants to be in her village again in the future. In other words, she doesn't want to break away from the past, which gives her the power to be in the mind. According to Bergson, real time is the inner life of a person. One can experience the past, present and future at the same time. However, what she lived in now has passed again. Agustinus states that when the things that existed in the past are remembered or remembered or told, the image of the narrated is seen in the present because they are still in the memory (Bergson, 2015: 26). The most obvious example of this in the documentary is the walnut tree. It reminds both the past and the present.

Time is the perception of the change in human consciousness and soul. There are two types of tenses in real life. While the first is time that progresses in real life in chronological order and is irreversible, the second is the non-chronological time that we go back and forth through our memory in the past, present and future. That is the real time (Yilmaz, 2011: 62-64). According to Bergson, now is an extension of the past. Bergson defines memory as a reality that completely preserves the past and expresses that it will spontaneously pass from the hills of the past to the present "I". According to him, remembering is the fact that the past should come spontaneously and fuse into the present (Bergson, 1998: 17-18). Just like Habibe, her sister and Derdo's conversations about the past, family members remembering and talking about their arrival in Istanbul upon the questions of the director on New Year's Eve in Istanbul, and the relatives in Yerevan voicing their memories of Anatolia.

Throughout the documentary, we do not only witness the remembrance of the Kumk village Armenians, the attitude of the village inhabitants towards the Armenians is closely related to how they remember them. Derdo tells that a peasant does not want to sell her butter. These three Armenian women, who lived far from the center of the village, are not fully accepted by the villagers. There are also villagers who meet with them; Those who put a distance and think that nothing will be bought from the Armenians, nothing will be sold to them. This shows that the knowledge that they once lived with Armenians was pushed deep into the peasant's collective memory. There is no absolute forgetting. Dreams that have nothing to do with the way of life are pushed into the subconscious. Remembered things live in memory and thus interact with the present (Yılmaz as cited in Ulken:67). Onal says that during the documentary filming, those who came from the center of the village thought they were there to remove the burials of Armenians (Onal, 2020). While there are possible burials left behind by the Armenians in the memory of the villagers, what Derdo remembers is about a past full of pain, difficulty and loss.

It is much more real and continuous than the time lived in the past. Time does not disappear without a trace. According to Bergson, the time lived in is not only the continuation of individual moments, but also the changes in human consciousness and soul. Bergson talks about subjective time here. The subjective time varies depending on the culture and experiences of the person. In other words, it states that when a person does not live in time, time lives in a person. Memories and what is experienced in the present are intertwined (Yilmaz: 66-76). Memories of our own emotions almost always play a role in the formation and structuring of our personal identity. In particular, our identity as individuals and our ability to predict our future behavior is based in part on our memories of emotional responses to previous events (in Ricoeur's book, Lambert et al: 253).

Derdo, whose house and land were confiscated after her husband was murdered, while telling the past, "If this was my mind then ... what would I do if this language was in my mouth. I had nothing left. Neither my house, nor my soil, nor fork nor duvet ..." she says. According to Onal, this sentence of Derdo is that the fear and timidity of the past gave way to comfort. Derdo now feels more comfortable to speak and tell, partly because she has learned Turkish. Derdo, who now comfortably expresses her past and her experiences, tends to worry about her neighbors with whom she suffers the same common pain, while sharing her memories and past with the audience through the documentary (Onal, 2020). In this sense, the documentary becomes a platform where Derdo shares the memories she shared with her relatives, whom she suffered similarly, with others who have never seen it before.

Documentary as a Counter-Hegemony Platform

According to Eagleton, Gramsci defines hegemony as the way a ruling power obtains the consent of the people it commands to strengthen its rule. The content of the word includes both consent and pressure (Terry, 1996: 12). With hegemony, the conflicts in society are drawn to the safe haven of ideology and consensus is achieved and ended. For the continuation of the environment of consent and reconciliation, in other words, the continuity of the safe harbor, hegemony must be maintained. The process in question is not a simple and ordinary process of establishing power. It takes place through mutual resistance and at the same time cooperation between the ruling class and groups and the classes and groups subject to it, always through negotiation. While hegemony is defined as the way of governing the society with the consent of the lower classes in unequal class relations, the most important area where consent is gained is the cultural field. The hegemony established by pressure and coercion in totalitarian societies is established through propaganda and promotion in contemporary societies (Caglar, 2019: 2-3).

In every environment where the forms of government emerge and power relations are experienced, how to obtain consent and social consensus, how to achieve hegemony, and how to expand the area of power is a fundamental problem. The existence and continuation of power in totalitarian and oppressive authoritarian societies have been seen on the stage of history for many years. However, in today's world where pluralist understanding has developed and democratic gains are increasing, the legitimacy and continuity of the government requires ideological fields. In other words, power is not just a political factor. Dominance should be ensured in all areas of social and cultural life. The effect of cinematic products is inevitable in the relations of self-consensual ideological superiority, control and direction between social classes or groups. The idea of hegemony, predicted by Gramsci, connects the society within the framework of the dominant ideology, acts as a phenomenon that unifies and brings them together, and restructures all institutions in line with its own id eology (Ayhan and Eda, 2014: 1-33).

On the other hand, it should not be forgotten that hegemony is never a complete situation. If we accept hegemony as the use of ideology as a legitimization tool, hegemony is realized by placing the dominant political system in the minds of individuals who make up the society through ideology. On the other hand, those who aim for social transformation should be able to correctly analyze the class relations and social power relations of the society they are in (Ataay & Kalfa, 2008, p: 37 as cited in Gurbuz). While discussing the concept of hegemony, those aiming at transformation should look at ideology only in terms of class and economy. Apart from this, the concepts of genre, race, gender and class should also be taken into consideration. Basically defined economically, hegemony is also the political, cultural and ideological rule of the ruling class over society. But this power of hegemony does not always proceed in a fixed balance (Coban, 2003: 162). The realization of this function by the narrators, the inclusion of representations for the change of existing patterns in the narratives, and the initiation of the change of existing myths in the cultural field bring social change (Aktas, 2018: 97). According to Gramsci, the basic condition of all kinds of political and socio-economic historical transformation and the strategy set out for this purpose is the manifestation of a collective will in this direction (Gramsci, 1989: 165). Only with the counter-hegemony to be developed in this way, cultural social cohesion is ensured by integrating around an equal and common world view.

Cinema, which can use persuasiveness thanks to its similarity to reality, is an effective propaganda tool in this respect. Cinema, which plays a major role in the upholding of existing myths, enables the audience to identify with what they see on the screen, thanks to the techniques it uses. Through cinema, we can have positive or negative evaluations about events that we have never experienced, whether personal or historical. However, instead of changing the existing, it ensures that the viewer remains passive by experiencing catharsis, and the world is confirmed and reaffirmed as it is. The function of myths that are reaffirmed through cinema is to spread the dominant ideology. The dominant ideology, on the other hand, maintains its existence through the repeated presentation of stereotypes about concepts such as gender, race, and class, which exist in society and the continuation of this existence is consciously provided. The success of the ruling class is that it presents what is in its own interest as if it is in the benefit of the whole society and manages to cover up reality. The function of cinema and other cultural narratives is important in creating the mentioned social reality and creating the desired change through representations. There are cases where different classes, races and ethnicities are not represented or cannot represent themselves even if they are. Identities formed through representation as well as the representation of different classes are also the determinants of society. Cinema is the representation arena of such struggles. It serves the change processes as well as the protection of the existing system (Aktas, 2018: 99).

Cinema introduces us to the world we live in, brings us face to face with the things we fear, and often forces us to compare with the events of real life and the thoughts we have on these events (Ilbuga, 2019: 3). In other words, cinema, which can be evaluated as a representation of social life, can raise awareness in the society while critically questioning ideologies that produce false consciousness (Deniz and Akmese, 2015: 87). Past experiences are shaped in consciousness as memories of the person. And these memories are presented to the audience through the cinema. Documentary is the most important cinematic product in which memories are presented with all their authenticity, according to the definition specified in the meeting held by pioneers in the field of documentary in Czechoslovakia in 1948. According to that, documentary film, with all the methods of recording on celluloid, the interpretation of any aspect of reality, creating a sensation or reason with shots or formations based on events, expanding human knowledge and understanding, offering solutions and stimulating the economy, culture and human relations. (Rotha, 1995: 21).

Turkey Documentarian Union, connects all the elements of civil culture with the need to be maintained documentary cinema (Sonmez, 1997: 260). Oskay described documentary as; It sees it as a field of art that resists the forgetfulness, despair and ruthlessness arising from the relationships that people establish with nature or with other people (Oskay, 1997: 48). One of the main functions of documentary cinema, which has always used its frame in favor of people and society, is to carry the stories of the groups that are invisible, left silent, marginalized and ignored into the future. When this conscious and moral responsibility correctly realizes the conscience-bearing feature of the eye, the documentary becomes one of the tools to fulfill an important task in coexistence, peace building, protection and memory building. Asks questions, searches for answers, offers solutions. Visual narratives and components of narratives include the possibilities of producing a counter discourse as well as means that imaginations can be used, manipulated and controlled by powers. For this reason, documentaries try to break the existing language of the mainstream media, which tends to construct society in certain ways every day, with the voice and eyes of hegemony (Susam: 8).

Onal says that documentary can be a tool of counter-hegemony against the dominant discourse. Where the documentary itself in the process of pulling the Armenians in Turkey and Onal, indicating that a learning process of how they live, when he learned that Mary grandaughter of Derdo, is from Bitlis, was very surprised. According to him, Armenians live in Istanbul, there are no Armenians living in the East. After this astonishment, Onal, who listens to the story of Derdo, states that a woman has decided to document her struggle against the system and the aghas there for her land (Onal, 2020).

On the other hand, the interaction of the director with the audience is not only due to aesthetic concern but mostly to take an approach to give a message, to direct or to create a space of hegemony against social and ideological hegemony. The documentary aims to show everything as it is, not as it seems. Using reality instead of fiction means understanding the relationships of people with the society they live in. The documentary film medium, which aims to convey reality, is quite suitable to be used as a counter-hegemony field with this feature. However, documentary film directors often say things that do not pose a risk to them. However, the field of the documentary is wider. Taking risks comes about by saying things that were not said and wanted not to be said (Hakan, 2018: 48). Those who are not wanted to be told are voiced, documented and recorded. According to Ricouer, documenting is also a witness. The documentary wants us to witness what happened. The word "I was there", the typical expression of testimony, comes from this match. What has been proven is both the reality of past things and the simultaneous presence of the narrator at the scene (Ricoeur: 185).

Drawing attention to the recording function of the documentary, Onal says that thanks to this documentary, Derdo's past was recorded. On the other hand, the documentary life is not only the person whose life is recorded, but also the one who interprets it.

The documentary filmmaker, who deals with the conflicts encountered in the society, has a say and responsibility on important issues such as what should be emphasized, which question should be addressed and questioned. From this point of view, we can say that creating a public opinion about guiding the future as much as questioning the past is among the obligations of the documentarian (Susam, 2015: 130). The documentary genre of cinema (Kuhn et al., 2017: 5), which itself can be seen as a memory storage or archive, can help the audience to confirm, question and change their thoughts. In other words, documentary productions appear as products that can change our thinking and enable us to look at many issues with new approaches (Rotha, p: 91). Onal states that it is the director's duty to at least break the negative thoughts of his environment. It therefore emphasizes the desire to convey a real life story without agitation, hoping to be able to change the views of ministers who are strict and distant to ethnic differences. He mentions that the prejudices of many people who find the story real and different are also broken (Onal, 2020).

Conclusion

An important indicator of hegemony should be sought in the invisible censorship of the media. The regulation of statements or silence (non-representation) is nothing more than the censorship imposed by the media structure and functioning on media content. The cultural inclusiveness of the media and the fact that the cultural field is made by neoliberal ideology necessitate a collective struggle in every field (Tekinalp and Ruhdan, 2006: 174). We can say that, in Turkey the recent documentaries of all kinds away from restrictive identification, the locality, the language, the culture and discussed issues on ideology and taking from this point, the documentary against mainstream media could be considered as an alternative to informed sources and being able to develop different interpretations of reality that we were in. While the voiceless groups gain visibility through the documentary, thanks to this visibility, they find the opportunity to express themselves rather than being represented by different perspectives. Thus, the relationship established with memory has the opportunity to expand into a more democratic, dynamic and positive field.

This possibility opens up a field of struggle for the discourse shaped within the framework of the dominant ideology with various manipulation techniques and creates a counter-discourse practice by taking the relationship between images and memory as a reference (Susame: 15-19). In the documentary *Mother Derdo and the Walnut Tree* (Onal, 2016), the director opened a new area of resistance for Derdo, who had to leave the land where she was born and raised, because she was not given the right to live in her village and fulfilled the function of the documentary to remember and convey the past. Derdo, who does not have the opportunity to make her voice heard in the public, could told her past to al lot of audiences and the experiences of her relatives with whom she lived the same past, the traces left by the past on them and what they experienced today through the documentary. The documentary has turned into an area of counter-hegemony for Derdo and her relatives, who have suffered many difficulties in the past, lost her husband, land, had to migrate, were excluded, ignored, and carried the heavy burden of the past in her memory.

References

Aktas, S. (2018). "İdeolojik Bir Aygıt Olarak Sinema: "Top Gun Film Anlatisinda Egemen İdeolojinin Temsili". *Beykent Üniversitesi Sosyal Bilimler Dergisi*, 11 (2), 96-112.

Ataay, F., Kalfa C. (2008) "Modern Prens'ten 'Post-Modern Prens'e: Gramsci'nin Siyasal Parti Kuramı Üzerine". *Akdeniz İİBF Dergisi*, 8 (15), 26-49.

Aytekin, H. (2018). "Can Documentary Filmmakers Be a Parrhesiastes? A Glance of Documentary Film History in Turkey via Notion of "Telling the Truth". *Sinefilozofi*, 5 (3), 45-66.

Bergson, H. (1998). *Metafiziğe Giriş*, trans. Barış Karacasu. Ankara: Bilim ve Sanat Yayınları.

Bergson, H. (2015). *Madde ve Bellek*, trans. Işık Ergüden. Ankara: Dost Kitapevi.

Boyer, P., Wertsch V. J. (2011). *Zihinde ve Kültürde Bellek*, trans. Yonca Aşçı Dalar. İstanbul: İş Bankası Yayınları.

Caglar, B. (2019). *"Hegemony: An Encyclopedic Article from Antonio Gramsci on Stuart Hall (Hegemonya: Antonio Gramsci' den Stuart Hall'a Ansiklopedik Bir Makale"*, https://www.researchgate.net/publication/332901807_ [Access:20.03.2020]

Celikaslan, Ö. (2016). *"Hengri Bergson'un Zaman ve Bellek Kuramı: Bir Film İncelemesi Hiroşima Sevgilim"*, http://kirpi.fisek.com.tr/index.php?metinno=sinema/20060529082316.txt. [Access:20.02.2020]

Deleuze, G. (2005). *Bergsonculuk*, trans. Hakan Yücefer. İstanbul: Otonom.

Deniz, Z., Akmese K. (2015). "Sinemada Toplumsal Eşitsizliklerin Temsili: "Çoğunluk" Filmi Örneği". *Erciyes İletişim Dergisi "Akademia"*, 4, (1), 86-96.

Eagleton, T. (1996). *İdeoloji*, trans. Muttalip Özcan. İstanbul: Ayrıntı Yayınları.

Gramsci, A. (1984). *Modern Prens*, trans. Esin Pars. İstanbul: Birey ve Toplum Yayıncılık.

GRAMSCI, A. (1989) Selections from the Prison Notebooks, Londra, Lawrence and Wishart.

Ilbuga Ucar, E. *siegfried-kracauer/s=15531-Film Teorisi*, [Access: 20.03. 2019].

Kuhn, A., Biltereyst, D. Meers, P. (2017). "Memories of cinemagoing and film experience: An introduction". *Memory Studies*, 10 (1), 3–16.

Makal, O. (2014). *Sinemada Tarihin Görüntüsü*. İstanbul: Kalkedon Yayınları.

Oskay, U. (1997). "Belgesel Sinema, Ampirik Algılama ve 'Büyük Balık Küçük Balığı Yer! Dedirten Globalleşmenin Kültürü", Ed. Semra Güzel. *Belgesel Sinemacılar Birliği 1. Ulusal Konferansı Bildirileri* içinde. İstanbul: Tayf Basım.

Rotha, P. (1995). *Belgesel Sinema*, trans. İbrahim Şener. İstanbul: Sistem Yayıncılık.

Ricoeur P. (2012). *Hafıza, Tarih, Unutuş*, trs. Mehmet Emin Özcan. İstanbul: Metis Yayınları.

Sofuoğlu, H. (2004). "Bergson ve Sinema", *Selçuk İletişim Dergisi*. 3 (3), 66-76.

Sonmezcan, N. (1997). "Yola Çıkarken", Eds. Semra Güzel. *Belgesel Sinemacılar Birliği 1. Ulusal Konferansı Bildirileri* İçinde, İstanbul: Tayf Basım.

Susam, A. *Çatışmadan Barışa Belgesel Sinemanın İşlevi*, https://www.academia.edu/14118330/%C3%87at%C4%B1%C5%9Fmadan_Bar%C4%B1%-C5%9Fa_Belgesel_Sineman%C4%B1n_%C4%B0%C5%9Flev [Access: 20.03. 2020].

Susam, A. (2015). *Toplumsal Bellek ve Belgesel Sinema*. İstanbul: Ayrıntı Yayınları.

Tarkovski, A. (1986). *Mühürlenmiş Zaman*, trans. Mazlum Beyhan. İstanbul: Agora Yayıncılık.

Tekinalp, Ş., Uzun, R. (2006). *İletişim Araştırma ve Kuramları*. İstanbul: Beta Basım.

Van Dijk, T. A. (2003). *"Söylem ve İdeoloji: Mitoloji, Din, İdeoloji"*, trans. Nurcan Ateş, Barış Çoban ve Zeynep Özarslan. İstanbul: Su Yayınları.

Yilmaz, H. (2011). "Henri Bergson'un Zaman Kavramına Yaklaşımının Çağdaş Anlatı Sinemasına Etkisi". *Sosyal Bilimler Dergisi*, 13 (2), 62-78.

Other Resources:

Uskan, N. (Producer) and Onal, S. (Director). (2016). Mother Derdo and Walnut Tree, (Documentary). Turkey Istanbul.

FEEDBACK STRATEGIES AND E-ASSESSMENT IN ONLINE LEARNING

*Zafer GÜNEY**

Introduction

With the transmission of the Covid-19 virus and the emergence that the consequences were very severe, face-to-face education was interrupted in the world and distance education was initiated. In the past year, it is seen that the transition to face-to-face education may take longer than expected, with the emergence of different variants with the risk of faster transmission. Distance education courses, which have been passed quickly and urgently, have shown their effectiveness in learning and teaching processes for more than a year. It is seen that effective and efficient applications in the stages of instructional design, online course designs, content development, use of multimedia in order to achieve predetermined teaching goals and target behaviors are rapidly taking place in the learning process. On the other hand, evaluation and giving feedback, which is an important part of the teaching processes, tries to catch up with this speed in order to reach the learning goals in an effective and reliable way.

Today, technology has been used in all areas of life and has taken an indispensable form by facilitating human life. Individuals must have a certain level of knowledge and skills in order for people to understand technology and take advantage of the opportunities it provides (Baki et al., 2009; Karataş et al., 2016; Oral, 2004). In

---

* Assist. Prof. Dr. Faculty of Education, Computer and Instructional Technologies Education, Istanbul Aydin University, Istanbul, Turkey, https://orcid.org/0000-0003-1974-4264.

order to achieve predetermined goals and achieve success in distance education environments where technology is used extensively, it is aimed to achieve the target gains of learners by giving tasks such as research, homework, projects or creating a scenario.

The importance and quantity of the studies carried out by the learners in order to achieve these goals cannot be denied whether these studies provide the expected outputs in line with the objectives, and whether the studies have reached the pre-determined level. Without evaluating the work done by the students about the tasks they have taken, such as homework and projects, it will appear as not correcting the mistakes and errors, carrying the same mistakes and deficiencies with the student and repeating the same mistakes in the next process. In this direction, this process, which can be called as the activity performance of the students such as homework and projects, should be provided with feedback. We can define it as the process of informing the student about the mistakes, mistakes, incompleteness and achievements made by different individuals, such as teachers or peers, regarding the work and projects of students regarding the tasks given feedback in the teaching process (Nicol & Macfarlane Dick, 2006).

In order to reach the predetermined goals and target behaviors, it is necessary to give feedback as to whether the work done by the students is at the expected level, if it is more than expected, it is necessary to use a reinforcer, or if it is lower than expected, it is necessary to report mistakes and errors, and to indicate the deficiencies (Hattie & Timperley, 2007). In this direction, the purpose of the feedback is not only to confirm whether the work is correct or incorrect, (Boud & Malloy, 2013) but also to explain and guide what should be used in order to perform the task better (Shute, 2008).

Materials and Methods

Qualitative research model was adopted in this study, which examines the use of e-assessment and e-feedback in distance education. Qualitative research (Yıldırım & Şimşek, 2006) is a research method in which a qualitative process is adopted to collect data and determine perceptions and events in a natural and holistic way in the natural environment of observation and interview. Document analysis technique was used to collect data.

Evaluation in Terms of Teaching

Measurement is the numerical and symbolic expression of the result of the observation of information and behaviors that alone do not indicate directional judgment. Evaluation, on the other hand, can be explained as the decision, value judgment, and interpretation resulting from the comparison of the measurements with the predetermined criteria (Turgut & Baykul, 2012). In the evaluation process, teacher opinion, student ability, student's improvement (achievement), average success of the class, target behaviors are the main pillars and elements that have an important place. In addition, three types can be mentioned for the purpose of evaluation (Özçelik, 2011; Tekin, 2012; Bayrak & Yurdugül 2015).

a. In the assessment aimed at determining the level, it is aimed to measure the preliminary information and to reveal the level of readiness.

b. The goal of the evaluation of learning processes for monitoring and evaluation and shaping is to increase success. In this direction, feedback is provided to the students in the form of guiding, learning, determining their mistakes and deficiencies, and giving tendencies, by revealing the performance processes of the students and improving them (Sadler, 1989). The goal of determining the learning outcomes of students is not an evaluation for the grading system, but rather to provide information.

c. Aiming to determine the learning level by determining student success; Evaluation of performance such as selection, grading (report card grades), certificate, diploma, qualification documents, certification of learning competence, ranking (Sadler, 1989).

The subject that needs to be focused on in evaluating according to purpose is monitoring and formatting supported evaluations, which can be used much more effectively by employing technological opportunities (Doğan, 2020).

Curriculums are generally planned in a hierarchical structure, from easy to difficult, from simple to complex, at the stage of structuring the lessons. The subjects that were explained before are important in terms of forming the basis for the following subjects. For this, mistakes and mistakes must be stated in a timely, effective, clear and high quality manner. Otherwise, the deficiencies and errors that occur during the learning process or the course period accumulate and cause the problems to increase at the end of the process. Therefore, evaluations should be made at the end of the sections and feedback should be given without wasting time. In practice, it is seen that evaluations for monitoring, shaping and directing the learning are not used much during the evaluation of learning, mostly for appraisal, session-based exams that determine the situation such as midterm and final report are applied (Doğan, 2020). As a result of this, the student carries his mistakes to the end of the semester since no feedback is given about his deficiencies and mistakes, and these evaluation deficiencies are among the reasons for the failure.

Traditional Assessment Approaches

They can also be used in online education. They are the most used methods in traditional evaluation processes for a long time. Uses conventional questions that evaluate the learner levels of achievement differently from their development, keeping the teaching process separate from the evaluation phase (Tekindal, 2014). In this context, the goal of the measurement and appraisal process is perceived as grading students. In measurement, multiple-choice items (widely used in high school and after), true-false items, matching items, gap-filling questions, open-ended questions, written, short-answer exams, homework and projects, and oral exams are included.

Alternative Assessment Approaches / Complementary Assessment Tools and Methods (Özen, 2019)

There are many approaches in the literature and they can also be used in online education.

a. Self assessment

b. Peer Review

c. Performance evaluation (Checklists or Ranking Scales)

d. Rubric

e. Product (Portfolio - Personal Development Files)

f. Learning Diaries

g. Structured Grid I. Word Association Tests

h. Concept Maps

j. Diagnostic Branched Tree

k. Verbal Fluency Tests

l. Demonstration, Anecdote, Discussion, Exhibition, Observation, Interview (Interview), Project, Homework, Research Paper

Wills et al. (2008) highlighted 16 types of question items that can be used online. Different from the above; It refers to the items of inline choice, associate, order, textentry, select point, file upload. Multiple choice question types are preferred more, especially because of the high number of students in higher education and the rapid analysis and feedback with the help of information systems (Nicol, 2007).

Table 1. Traditional and New Generation Evaluation Features (Adapted from Özen 2019)

	Traditional assessment	E-evaluation
Time	At the end of learning and teaching processes	Integrated with the process, at every stage of the process
Process	Linear	Adaptable
Feedback	After the evaluation	Instantly
Substances	General	Advanced
Accessibility	Limited	Universal designed

In the e-evaluation process, it is necessary to analyze and analyze the data to be taken into account in the planning of education, and to give the students timely feedback, which is one of the indicators of learning and teaching stages. When the students are viewed in terms of reporting the difference between the predetermined goals and behaviors and the student's achievements, it has a regulatory effect in the learning process as the student will make an effort to close and reduce this difference (Black and Wiliam, 1998). Butler, Karpicke and Roediger (2008) proved in their research that the feedbacks have an effect on correcting the errors originating from memory. They found that they have an organizing feature for the feedbacks and that the feedbacks indicating the correct option are effective in correcting the mistakes of the wrongly solved questions. It was concluded that the feedbacks explained in the questions answered without being fully sure and doubled the recall. On the basis of this, it can be stated that the feedback given on time and for verification is effective on the learning processes according to the environments where feedback is not received.

E-Evaluation

While the innovations in information technologies have changed the process, structure and quality of learning environments, they have also brought innovations and speed to the evaluation process. Assessment processes are mostly implemented in groups, depending on the session, in the form of an exam, using paper and pencil, and in a habitual way to identify the learning process. With the rapid developments in information technologies, it is possible to select, scroll, write, upload files on the screen, regardless of session and time. With the interactions and the learning process, different assessment environments (individual, test, item, etc.) have also started to be used. The modern perspective on teaching technologies has also started with a calculator that includes these three features (Holmes and Gardner, 2006).

E-evaluation can be defined as applying the types and ways of evaluation together with information technologies in order to reach predetermined goals and determine the level of acquiring knowledge, skills and acquisitions (Shute & Kim, 2012). JISC (2007) explained e-assessment as the use of information and communication tools in the process of communicating and interacting with students, from recording assignments, projects, research and assignments to their conclusion. The steps in the instructional evaluation process are also included at this stage (Doğan, 2020).

E-evaluation, in which information technologies can be used effectively, quickly and on time, is e-evaluation that aims to formulate and evaluate the type that is frequently used when considered according to the purposes. E-assessment environments that are set forth for learning teaching processes generally aim to monitor and formulate. Using e-evaluation methods and tools; It provides opportunities such as analysis of exams, reaching instant results, developing and applying tests independently of time, reaching large groups easily, providing instant feedback specific to the assignments (Vasilyeva et al., 2007).

Since informatics and internet technologies will be used quickly and effectively. Wmothile conducting e-evaluation, many quantitative and qualitative data (item difficulties, taxonomy, information diversity, explanation of correct answers, detailed feedback, etc.) can be created immediately for the evaluation process. As a result of the exam or measurement phase, instant feedback can be provided to the deficiencies and errors.

In order to give the feedback on time by using the exam results, one of the test statistics; Item statistics such as test average, average difficulty, variance, reliability, and frequency distributions also include item difficulty, item discrimination power, analysis of options (for multiple-choice questions), rate of leaving the item blank. analyzes available immediately (Doğan, 2020).

Table.2 Sample İtem and Test Statistics

Student Number:	Question1	Question2	Question3	Question4	Question5	Question6
111	+	-	+	-	-	+
112	+	-	-	-	-	+
113	+	-	+	-	-	+
114	+	-	+	-	+	+

The table above can be created immediately after the exam, such as item and test statistics, and this table indicates that the (+) behavior has gained. (-) the behavior and the acquisition have not been learned sufficiently. For the questions that the student answers incorrectly, tasks, homework and projects can be given to complete the deficiencies, and timely feedback can be given to correct their mistakes. In the event that a large number of students or entire classes give incorrect answers to a question item (such as the example of question 2 and question 4), it can be inferred that the behavior or achievement measured by the question has not been adequately taught, i.e. either we could not teach, or our curriculum scope was not trained, or it could not be achieved because it was not explained in accordance with the students' level. we can say. Accordingly, new study activities can be planned for the whole class. While giving feedback to the group, we also provide feedback for ourselves.

Advantages of the E-Evaluation System

It is an evaluation approach suitable for e-learning that accelerates the measurement and evaluation system. Students can be provided instant feedback. Results based on absolute criteria can be reached more quickly. It allows the use and evaluation of almost all traditional exam types. Text writing areas (textarea) can be used to answer written exams. Facilitates data analysis, enables quick and immediate evaluation results (Vasilyeva et al., 2007; Doğan, 2020; Keskin, 2019).

In short-answer tests, simple text input can be used to get answers remotely. It can be used for selection boxes, scroll list, multiple choice questions, true and false questions. Many exams on the Internet have been prepared with this method. A single exam can be created by combining different exams. The information system can select, measure, evaluate items randomly with the questions in the pool when needed, and automatically transfer them to the grade lists. The validity and reliability examinations of the items are done instantly (item difficulty level, item discrimination power, etc.) (Doğan, 2020). Analysis of the answers can be done as soon as the exams are finished (average, success rate, etc.). Its cost is low. Space and time constraints are eliminated (Doğan, 2020; Keskin, 2019). If the evaluation period is not fixed, students can take the exam whenever and wherever they want. Measurement and evaluation results can be reported online. More visuals can be included in the questions. Using animations, more realistic conditions can be created compared to classical exams. Records can be reviewed later, simulations that are close to real life can be offered to students. Performance evaluation can be made with software that enables experimentation. New possibilities of interaction can be provided. Multimedia elements can be used. It can allow evaluations to be stored and used for comparison with future ones. Assessment questions or options can be presented to students by mixing them in a way that looks different for each student.

Disadvantages;

The main ones are the problem of access, plagiarism and cheating, someone else doing the task that the student has to do. For example, even if the student answers the question correctly, the process steps may not be shown in the design of the questions asked. Some of the disadvantages are listed below (Doğan, 2020).

a. Teachers and students must be computer literate.

b. Internet infrastructure must be sufficient.

c. Maintaining internet security can be difficult and costly.

d. Measurement and evaluation software may not be sufficient in terms of capacity.

e. Software may not be user friendly.

f. Web server is needed.

g. Servers require operating systems.

h. Web service is required for publishing the exams on the web.

i. A database is needed to keep the records.

j. In the processing and storage of user data, applications such as ASP, PHP, JSP are required to be installed and maintained.

Online Feedback in Learning

As it is used in every stage of the learning process, feedbacks (feedback) are included in the evaluation process. These are the results that emerge with student evaluations and show the gains based on student performance and direct the teaching stages (Narciss, 2008). With the feedback, the learning process is created for the students in different ways. Feedbacks have functions that can be considered as directing, motivating and affirming and reinforcing (Çalışkan, 2015). In fact, the existence of bringing back effects in mind such as the achievement and permanence of giving feedback has been revealed. (Kang, McDermott, & Roediger III, 2007).

E-Feedbacks are information that reveal the mistakes and deficiencies of different individuals such as teachers and peers about the work they have done to students or whether they have reached the predetermined goals, knowledge and behaviors through online environments (Hattie and Timperley, 2007) In the feedbacks, the differences between the goals and achievements and the studies performed are explained in a simple level. For this reason, it is expected to express how to eliminate mistakes and deficiencies by revealing them. It is known that feedback has a critical importance in the evaluation phase and is an important process that needs to be implemented. (Bloxham & Boyd, 2007). In this context, Hattie and Jaeger (1998) stated that supporting the tasks, projects and assignments directed to students with feedbacks is effective and contributes to learning. While the feedbacks given during the learning process are expressed as formative feedbacks, the feedbacks given at the end of the process are described as summative feedbacks (Sadler, 1989).

Narciss (2008) states in the studies in the literature that feedback has many features such as strengthening, informative, motivating, guiding, regulatory, instructive, reinforcing, guiding, evaluating, confirming, giving suggestions, showing differences, and reconstructing the learning process.

Kulhavy and Wager (1993) pointed out the stages of motivation, reinforcement and informing about the purpose of providing feedback. These properties, which they identify as the feedback triangle (Figure 1), explain the three functions of the feedback. Feedback; It aims to increase the success rate of the answers and as motivating and reinforcing information in the face of correct answers;

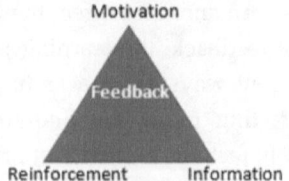

Figure 1. Three Functions the Feedback (Kulhavy and Wager, 1993)

Grouping related to feedback usually arises in terms of content. Types are shown as simple feedback (confirmatory: true / false, test result information) and detailed feedback according to their content. According to the complexity of the content in the literature, it has been classified by Kulhavy and Stock (1989) and this distinction has been explained in detail by Shute (2008) as follows.

Table 3. Feedback types (Shute, 2008) (simple to complex)

Feedback Type	Definition
No feedback	There is no indication of the correctness of the student's answer.
Verification	It is also called the knowledge of results (KS). Information about the accuracy of the individual's answer / s is provided. For example correct response rate, wrong, right etc. No information is given as to what the correct answer is.
Correct answer	It is also called the knowledge of correctresponse. No additional explanations are provided for correct answer information
Retry	(repeat-until-correct feedback), When the wrong answer is given, the individual is informed, the individual has the right to attempt one or more answers to the question.
Flagging the wrong	It is also called the location of mistakes (LM), mistakes in the solution are marked, the correct answer is not given.
Detailed	Includes an explanation of why the particular answer is correct, allowing students to repeat the relevant topic. Correct answer information may also be provided. Six types of detailed feedback are explained below.
Attribute oriented	It is a detailed feedback type that presents the basic characteristics of the concepts or skills being learned.
Subject oriented	The detailed feedback type that provides information on the subject.
Response oriented	It is a detailed feedback on a particular answer that explains why the error is wrong and why the correct answer is correct.
Tips / Routers	It is the presentation of detailed feedback information to the learners to find the correct answer without clearly sharing the correct answer information. Explanation of the next step, examples with solutions, strategic guides etc.
Debugging / Misconceptions	Learners are informed about their misconceptions and mistakes. The type of feedback for error analysis and elaboration.
Informative instructional feedback	Informative instructional feedback is the presentation of metacognitive and strategic information for the completion of the learning task to learners without sharing the correct answer. The correct answer is usually not given. However, emphasis is made on the wrong. It is the most comprehensive type of feedback.

Gouli et al. (2006) classified the types of feedback as informative, educational and reflective feedback types. Informative feedback is a type of feedback that involves informing the learner whether his response or performance is right or wrong. Educational feedback is a type of feedback that refers to the review of the relevant parts of the learning material in order to ensure that the learner can give the correct answer. Reflective feedback is one that encourages the student to reflect on his / her responses and think about the reasons for his / her mistakes. In another study, Blignaut and Trollip (2003) discussed the types of feedback in three categories as corrective, informative and socratic feedbacks. Corrective feedback is defined as the type of feedback that includes correcting the errors in the content of the student's answer to the question. Informative feedback is a feedback presented from a more explanatory perspective on the accuracy of the student's response in the learning task. Socratic feedback is specified as the type of feedback that asks the student reflective questions about the answer given on the learning task. Some of the results obtained regarding the quality and effectiveness of the feedback are given below.

Table 4 Results Reached About Feedback Quality

Feedback Quality	Fast and on time Gibbs 1999; Gibbs and Simpson (2004)
	Intelligibility Mulliner & Tucker (2017)
	Detail, Specificity (Special feature) Mory (2004)
	Behavioral / not personal Jackson, et al (2015)
	Balanced, Specific, Generates action plan, Behavioral / not personal, Pays attention to learning climate, Quantifiable, Objective, Based on goals, Helpful / constructive, Modifiable traits Jackson, et al (2015)
	Emphasizing Positive Aspects / Useful / Constructive Jackson, et al (2015)
	Including the ongoing dialogue Merry et al. (2013)
	Stimulating, motivating and constructive Nicol and Macfarlane-Dick (2006)

Hattie and Timperley (2007), for feedback to be effective, it must be given towards the target (feed up), for the confirmation of the result (feed back) and for detail (feed forward). If it is goal-oriented, it is expected that the student will provide feedback in a structure that gives information about the goals, from what angle the student will view the study. For the approval of the result, that is, the feedback given for the purpose of verification is provided by considering the work done by the student, the current state of the study and the stage of the process.

In the elaboration stage, the student is informed about the next stages and the feedback he / she needs to improve performance is given. From the timing aspect, feedbacks are treated as postponed feedback with fast feedback (Shute, 2008). In rapid feedback, feedback is given to the student or learner in a corrective form as quickly as possible during each practice, test, application, question in the teaching process. In the case of postponed feedback, the feedback is given after the completion of the process, ie applications such as tests, practice and exams. On the other hand, Shute (2008) stated that postponed or delayed feedback for the time of feedback is metacognitive as well as motivating students' cognitive processes.

Many different ways can be considered in conveying the feedback processes to the students. To give an example of this, in files to be prepared similar to the question pool for feedback, one or more written ready feedbacks for each question can be provided automatically when the question is answered incorrectly in video, audio, written forms. The attention of the student may be negatively affected by the audible feedback in the assessment performed as an exam session (Heppleston et al., 2011).

Nicol and Macfarlane Dick (2006) set seven rules for external feedback on self-regulation, while Nicol (2009) brought these principles to twelve as follows:

1. Description of good performance (purpose, standards and criteria)

2. Directing to interesting learning tasks such as homework, projects and research.

3. Provide quality feedback to support students for self-verification purposes.

4. Allowing the structuring of corrections based on feedbacks

5. Clearly determining the contribution of evaluations such as grading, certificate and diploma to learning.

6. Directing to peer and teacher interaction in terms of communication

7. Giving importance to self-assessment and reflection in the learning process

8. Determining optional situations for the ratio of the subject, method and determined criteria in the evaluation process

9. Including students in the assessment process

10. Supporting the development of students

11. Positive motivation and orientation towards positive psycholog

12. Providing feedback for the improvement of learning and teaching processes

Conclusion

Measuring and evaluating the achievement of the educational objectives should be seen as a complementary element of the education (National Council Teachers of Mathematics, 2002). E-evaluation and e-feedback take place in the teaching and learning process in line with the rapid changes in information technologies.

Before the homework, research and projects given to the students, the evaluation rules are clearly given in the test instruction. (purpose, duration, rules and constraints, how many times will be granted in delivery, how and in what format it should be text / audio / picture / video, pptx / pdf / mp4 etc.) Guiding, motivating and reinforcing feedback can be used in the learning-teaching process. In cases where success and competence are noticed, the motivation of the successful students can be increased with reinforcers. Praise can be considered as an encouraging part of the evaluation. It can also be said that this situation will make teacher-student communication more effective.

There are studies that the most effective of different types of feedback, including text, audio, video, text video, audio video, text and audio video, is perceived as video (Setting, 2009). Although there are many studies on the effectiveness of teachers' feedback, it has been observed that peer feedback significantly increases student achievement (Can, 2019; Kılıç, 2019). Feedback varies according to many variables.

It is seen that e-evaluation processes have many advantages, which are mentioned above, with the effect of rapid changes in technology. It is important to benefit from these advantages in teaching processes. Feedback; It is of great importance among the tools teachers use to direct learners to predetermined learning goals and behaviors. Gibbs and Simpson (2004) stated in the feedbacks the importance of timing and being clear, understandable and dynamic for the purposes of learning process. Likewise, Mason and Burining (2001) stated that feedbacks can make changes on the mental activities of the student during the learning phase, and support the creation of new strategies. In this way, learners can see how close they can get to goals and behaviors with their newly created or improved perspectives.

Until recently, it was necessary to make some calculations, analyzes and spend time to make formative evaluation in the evaluation process, while the feedback and evaluation process can be carried out at the same time thanks to the technological developments in information systems. Information technologies have made the process much faster in the evaluation processes for monitoring and shaping, and timely feedback is very useful in seeing the mistakes and deficiencies of the students, increasing their motivation, and ensuring the repetition and permanence of what has been learned.

Suggestions

Teachers, who are in a guiding position in the learning process, should use the feedbacks effectively. Difficulties are encountered in controlling the evaluation process, especially in the evaluation of large groups. In these and similar situations, assigning research, projects, homework to learning groups with individual projects can provide success in achieving learning goals and behaviors.

The use of short-answer questions can be increased, and in blank-filling-type questions, students can be designed to answer by using their existing knowledge. Since the duration of the test can be determined as a whole, time limitations can be made for the question items. During the exam, individual questions can be shown to the student one by one. Returning to the answered or left blank question can be blocked. Option choices can be made randomly, that is, to appear in a different order to the students. The exam plan can be requested from the student in the form of solving the questions and taking pictures and uploading them to the exam system, or they can be asked to take their own video during the exam and upload them as a file attachment to the exam system. An exam similar to the traditionally used notebook book open application can be done, in this case, after the question is given, the student can make the research and upload the work requested from him to the exam system in a certain period of time. In such exams, students should be informed about how to do the work and how to submit it with rubrics previously tabulated. In word processing applications, it can be used in the feedback process by making changes such as explanation, correction, highlighting, and phosphorylation. Courses, in-service trainings and seminars can be organized to provide technological literacy to teachers and candidates. Learning analytics can be used to reveal the interactions of students during the course process.

Discussion forums / mediums can be used in the assessment and evaluation process. Similar to homework, projects and researches, it would be appropriate to plan discussion questions in accordance with previously determined goals and behaviors and to provide information about the evaluation process (such as tabulated rubric) to be formed at the beginning. Reinforcement-based approaches in the communication process can ensure a high level of interaction with the student. Questions, approved issues, and positive feedback should be reported to the student in the discussion forums. Students' criticism and positive evaluations of each other's work can also be considered.

In the use of questions in the test, similar questions should be used by grouping. Visuals and texts should not be used arbitrarily, as the use of visuals and text in the creation of questions should be used in situations where the student can use his knowledge and have an effect on solving the question in order to measure the student's achievements. Good questions should be as short as possible, concise, and consist of questions that can measure the behavior you want to measure without mixing variables, spoiling validity, and distracting the student. It will be appropriate to give feedbacks to all students participating in the assessment after the exam application is completed.

Feedback pools can be created by making groupings for each question. For each question, in case of an error, the feedback in the pool can be forwarded to the student who made the error by pulling the feedback directly from the database in which the pool is located, as the error occurs.

In this case, when the homework, projects and tasks related to the questions that have been answered incorrectly are coded in the functions of programming in a way that is specific to each item, automatic feedback about the question made incorrectly can be sent to the group one by one for each item.

References

Ayar, T. (2009). Öğretme-öğrenme sürecinde geri bildirim: Dördüncü ve beşinci sınıf öğretmen ve öğrencilerinin görüşlerine göre sınıfta geri bildirim kullanımının değerlendirilmesi.(Feedback in the teaching-learning process: Evaluation of the use of feedback in the classroom according to the opinions of fourth and fifth grade teachers and students) Unpublished Master's Thesis, Çukurova University, Institute of Education Sciences, Adana.

Baki, A., Yalçınkaya, H. A., Özpınar, İ. ve Çalık Uzun, S. (2009). Comparing views of primary school mathematics teachers and prospective mathematics teachers about instructional technologies. Turkish Journal of Computer and Mathematics Education (TURCOMAT), 1(1), 65-83.

Bayrak, Fatma & Yurdugül, Halil. (2015). e-değerlendirme ve e-dönüt, (e-evaluation and e-feedback,) Eğitim Teknolojileri Okumaları 2015, 22. chapter, Sakarya. Ed.: Buket Akkoyunlu, Aytekin İşman, Hatice Ferhan Odabaşı

Black, P., & Wiliam D. (1998). Assessment and classroom learning. assessment in education. Principles, Policy & Practice 5, no. 1

Blignaut, S., & Trollip, S. (2003). A taxonomy for faculty participation in asynchronous online discussions. In EdMedia + Innovate Learning (pp. 2043-2050). Association for the Advancement of Computing in Education (AACE).

Bloxham, S., & Boyd, P. (2007). Developing effective assessment in higher education: A practical guide. McGraw-Hill Education (UK).

Boud, D., & Molloy, E. (2013). Rethinking models of feedback for learning: the challenge of design. Assessment & Evaluation in Higher Education, 38(6), 698-712.

Butler, A.C., Karpicke, J.D., & Roediger III, H.L. (2008). Correcting a metacognitive error: feedback increases retention of low-confidence correct responces. Journal of Experimental Psychology: Learning, Memory and Cognition, 34(4). doi: 10.1037/0278-7393.34.4.918

Can, E. (2019). Yazılı Akran Dönüt Verme Eğitiminin Yabancı Dil Olarak İngilizce Öğrenen Türk Öğrencilerin Verdiği Dönütün Türüne ve Yazma Becerilerinin Gelişimine Etkisi.(The Effect of Written Peer Feedback Education on the Type of Feedback Given by Turkish Students Learning English as a Foreign Language and on the Development of Writing Skills) Anadolu University, Institute of Education Sciences, February 2019.

Çalışkan, M. (2015). Etkili Dönüt Verme Yolları (Ways Of Providing Effective Feedback). Turkish Studies, 10/11, 417-430. doi: http://dx.doi.org/10.7827/TurkishStudies.8613 (Retrieved: 15.05.2021).

Doğan, Nuri (2020). Uzaktan Öğretimde Ölçme Değerlendirme Yöntemleri, (Measurement and Evaluation Methods in Distance Education) Pearson Higher-Ed Webinars, 16.04.2020. https://www.youtube.com/watch?v=Ug--tViSUoI (Retrieved: 15.05.2021).

Gibbs G. & Claire Simpson. (2004). Conditions under which assessment supports students' learning. UK Learning and Teaching in Higher Education, Issue 1, 2004-05. Oxford University, 2 Open University.

Gouli, E., Gogoulou, A., Papanikolaou, K. A., & Grigoriadou, M. (2006). An adaptive feedback framework to support reflection, guiding and tutoring. In Advances in web-based education: Personalized learning environments

Hattie, J., & Jaeger, R. (1998). Assessment and classroom learning: A deductive approach. Assessment in Education: Principles, Policy & Practice, 5(1),

Hattie, J., & Timperley, H. (2007). Th e power of feedback. Review of Educational Research, 77(1), 81-112. doi: 10.3102/003465430298487

Hepplestone, S., Holden, G., Irwin, B., Parkin, H. J., & Th orpe, L. (2011): Using technology to encourage student engagement with feedback: A literature review. Research in Learning Technology, 19(2), 117-127. doi: 10.1080/21567069.2011.586677

Holmes, B., & Gardner, J. (2006). E-learning: Concepts and practice. Sage.

Jackson, J.L., Kay, C., Jackson, W.C. et al. (2015),The Quality of Written Feedback by Attendings of Internal Medicine Residents. J GEN INTERN MED 30, 973–978 (2015).https://doi.org/10.1007/s11606-015-32372

JISC-Joint Information Systems Comittee. (2010). Effective assesment in a digital age. Bristol: Higher Education Funding Council for England.

Kang, S. H., McDermott, K. B., & Roediger III, H. L. (2007). Test format and corrective feedback modify the effect of testing on long-term retention. European Journal of Cognitive Psychology, 19(4-5),

Karataş, S., Bozkurt, Ş. B. ve Hava, K. (2016). The perspective of history pre-service teachers' towards the use of digital storytelling in educational environments. Journal of Human Sciences, 13(1), 500-509.

Keskin, S. (2019). Uyarlanabilir Dönüt Sistemi Tasarımı İçin Kullanıcı Profillerinin Belirlenmesi.(Determining User Profiles for Adaptive Feedback System Design.)Hacettepe University, Unpublished PhD thesis Ankara

Kulhavy, R.W., & Stock, W.A. (1989). Feedback in Written Instruction: The Place of Response Certitude. Educational Psychology Review, 1(4).

Kulhavy, R.W., & Wager, W. (1993) 'Feedback in programmed instruction: historical context and implications for practice', in Dempsey, J.V. and Sales, G.C. (Eds.): Interactive Instruction and Feedback, Educational Technology, Englewood Cliffs, NJ

Kılıç, M. (2019). Akran Dönütü Öğretmen Dönütüne Karşı: Öğrencilerin Yazma Becerilerinde Söylem Belirleyicilerini Geliştirmek Üzerine Karşılaştırmalı Bir Vaka Çalışması.(Peer Feedback Versus Teacher Feedback: A Comparative Case Study on Developing Discourse Markers in Students' Writing Skills) Gazi University.

Mason, B. J., & Bruning, R. (2001). Providing feedback in computer-based instruction: what the research tells us. Retrieved February, 15, 2007.

Merry, S., M. Price, D. Carless, and M. Taras, eds. 2013. Reconceptualising Feedback in Higher Education: Developing Dialogue with Students. London: Routledge.

Mory, E. 2004. "Feedback Research Revisited." In Handbook of Research on Educational Communications and Technology, edited by D. Jonassen, 745–783. Mahwah, NJ Lawrence Erlbaum

Mulliner Emma & Tucker Matthew (2017) Feedback on feedback practice: perceptions of students and academics, Assessment & Evaluation in Higher Education, 42:2, 266-288, DOI: 10.1080/02602938.2015.1103365

Narciss, S. (2008). Feedback strategies for interactive learning tasks (Chapter 11). Handbook of research on educational communications and technology.

NationalCouncil of Teachers of Mathematics (2002). Principles and Standarts for school Mathematics. Virginia: NCTM Publications.

Nicol, D (2009). Transforming assessment and feedback: Enhancing integration and empowerment in the first year. Th e Quality Assurance Agency for Higher Education, Mansfield.

Nicol, D. (2007). Formative assessment and self‐regulated learning: a model and seven principles of good feedback practice. Studies İn Higher Education, 31, 199-218.

Nicol, D. J., & Macfarlane-Dick, D. (2006). Formative assessment and self-regulated learning: Amodel and seven principles of good feedback practice. Studies in Higher Education, 31(2),199-218. doi: 10.1080/ 03075070600572090

Oral, B. (2004). Öğretmen adaylarının internet kullanma durumları (Pre-service teachers' internet usage situations). XIII. National Educational Sciences Congress. Inönü University, Facultyof Education. Malatya.

Özçelik, D. A. (2011). Ölçme ve Değerlendirme (Measurement and Evaluation)(3.Ed). Pegem Akd, Ankara.

Özen, S.O. (2019). Öğrenenlerin e-değerlendirmeye dayalı kişiselleştirilmiş geri bildirim yollarının incelenmesi.(Examination of learners' personalized feedback based on e-assessment.) Unpublished Doctoral Thesis.

Özpinar, İ. (2017). Matematik öğretmeni adaylarının dijital öyküleme süreci ve dijital öykülerin öğretim ortamlarında kullanımına yönelik görüşleri. (The views of prospective mathematics teachers on the digital narrative process and the use of digital stories in teaching environments) Bartin University Journal of Faculty of Education, 6(3), 1189-1210.

Sadler, D. R. (1989). Formative assessment and the design of instructional systems. Instructional Science, 18, 119-144.

Shute, V. J. (2008). Focus on formative feedback. Review of Educational Research, 78(1), 153-189.

Shute, V. J., & Kim, Y. J. (2012). e-assessment. In N. Balacheff, J. Bourdeau, P. Kirschner, R. Sutherland, and J. Zeiliger (Eds.), TEL Thesaurus. Stellar Initiative. http://myweb.fsu.edu/vshute/pdf/eassessment.pdf (Retrieved: 15.05.2021).

Tekin, H. (2012). Eğitimde olcme ve değerlendirme (Measurement and evaluation in education)(21.Ed) Yargı publishing house: Ankara.

Tekindal, S. (2014). Okullarda Ölçme ve Değerlendirme Yöntemleri. (Measurement and Evaluation Methods in Schools) Ankara : Nobel Academy Publishing

Turgut, M. F., & Baykul, Y. (2012). Eğitimde Ölçme ve Değerlendirme (Measurement and Evaluation in Education) (6. Ed.). Ankara: Pegem Academy.

Vasilyeva, E., Puuronen, S., Pechenizkiy, M., & Rasanen, P. (2007). Feedback adaptation in web-based learning systems. International Journal of Continuing Engineering Education and Life Long Learning, 17(4/5), 337. DOI: 10.1504/IJCEELL.2007.015046.

WHO (World Health Organization), (2020). https://www.who.int/emergencies/diseases/novel-coronavirus-2019/question-and-answers-hub Son güncellenme tarihi 12 Ekim 2020, (Retrieved: 16.05.2021).

Wills, G., Kajaba, J., Argles, D., Gilbert, L., & Millard, D. (2008). Assessment delivery engine for QTIv2 tests. In: International CAA Conference, 8-9th July 2008, Loughborough UK.

Yıldırım, A. & Şimşek, H. (2006). Qualitative Research Methods in Social Sciences (5th Edition). Ankara: Seçkin Publishing.

IMPACT OF ORGANIZATIONAL CULTURE ON ORGANIZATIONAL INNOVATIVENESS: MODERATING EFFECT OF ORGANIZATIONAL POWER

*Mehmet KIZILOĞLU**

Introduction

Over the last half-century, there has been a significant change in the world. Nowadays, there are a number of new trends which are influencing the business of organizations both positively and negatively, such as globalization, intense competition and flattening of organizational structures. It is generally believed that there is a direct connection between such trends and changes, and these are actually resulted because of innovations. There is an importance of innovation on different levels, and there are a number of key reasons due to which organizational innovativeness is considered highly important (Taştan and Davoudi, 2017). Innovation in a country is considered as having a significant role in driving economic growth. It helps in improving the living standards as well as the welfare of people. With the help of organizations' trend towards innovation, individuals get an opportunity of making their life more comfortable. Nowadays, it has become highly important for organizations to focus on enhancing innovativeness as one of their core values. For this reason, they are required to focus on building that kind of organizational culture, where employees can

---

* Dr., Pamukkale University, Management and Organization, ORCID ID: orcid.org/0000-0002-6098-3980, mkiziloglu@pau.edu.tr.

be stimulated with challenging work and can be encouraged to share-worthy and creative ideas (Bankins et al., 2017)

In today's globalized and competitive business environment, it has become highly important for companies to focus on organizational innovativeness in order to get success. Innovation can prove to be much useful for stimulating the growth of an organization, specifically within the sports sector. The sports sector is one of the growing sectors in Turkey, so the focus of the current research study is on the sports sector of Turkey. There are many factors that can help in fostering organizational innovativeness, and organizational culture is one of those factors. It is important for the management of an organization to foster a corporate culture that is open to innovation. Besides this, organizational power bases are something that needs to be considered properly in order to enhance innovativeness in an organization (Lokuge et al., 2019). Previously, there have been very few studies conducted for empirically testing the relationship between organizational culture and organizational innovativeness (Shanker et al., 2017; Hwang and Choi, 2017). However, none of the prior studies focused on empirically testing such a relationship in the context of Turkish sports clubs. Besides this, none of the prior research studies investigated the moderating effect of key bases of organizational power on the relationship between organizational culture and organizational innovativeness. This research study has been carried out for investigating the impact of organizational culture on organizational innovativeness in the case of the Turkish sports' sector. Moreover, the key focus of this study is on testing how organizational power basis moderates the relationship between organizational culture and organizational innovativeness.

The aim of this study is to investigate the relationship between organizational culture and organizational innovativeness in the case of the Turkish sports' sector. The focus of this study is on achieving the following research objectives are; to investigate the importance of organizational culture for enhancing innovativeness in an organization in the Turkish sports' sector, to understand the link of organizational power bases with organizational innovativeness, to analyze the moderating effect of organizational power bases on the relationship between organizational culture and organizational innovativeness.

Literature Review

Organizational Culture

Even though there are various definitions of organizational culture, generally, it is defined as a set of values, norms and standards which make the core identity of a firm. In addition to this, it can also include a combination of beliefs and assumptions which shape management styles and processes within a company. An important role is played by organizational culture in the determination of working climate, strategy development, leadership style and key processes of an organization (Gemünden et al., 2018). It is highly important for the management of an organization to focus on its culture in order to make a difference. It helps in determining the relevance of features, organizational settings and core competencies by key members. Besides this, organizational culture is also used for defining the standards used for evaluating these characteristics (Erthal and Marques, 2018). Based on studies in the literature, it is found that strong corporate culture helps in improving the performance of an organization. This relationship can be direct or indirect, and it is linked with commitment as well as motivation fostered in individuals for dealing with key challenges and also for overcoming adversity. On the basis of a resource-based view, organizational culture is considered as a strategic resource that can be used for generating sustainable competitive advantage (Kraśnicka et al., 2018).

Organizational Innovativeness

Organizational innovativeness is an important capability that helps firms in gaining a competitive edge. It is defined as a process of commercialization that converts the idea to a new product or service. In order to ensure a high level of organizational innovativeness, it is highly important to have a new product, marketing method, process and organizational method, or it can include significant improvement in existing product, service or method (Ardi et al., 2020).

According to Ritala et al. (2020), organizational innovativeness is related to the capability of a firm to constantly developing and adopting new ideas, processes or products. With the help of organizational innovativeness, a company can become capable of dealing effectively with the turbulence of the external environment and hence, it is considered a key driver of long term success in business, specifically in the case of the dynamic business environment. In addition to this, Holtgrave et al. (2019) found that in challenging business environments, it is the responsibility of organizations to have the ability to cope with increasing complexity and high level of change. In such contexts, only those companies can get long term success which has the capacity of innovating and have the ability to respond to challenges in a faster way, as compared to non-innovative companies. Frega et al. (2018) claimed that innovativeness must be considered as multidimensional instead of unidimensional. It can include production or adoption as well as a process of exploiting value-added novelty. Hence, organizational innovativeness can be referred to as a process as well as an outcome. According to the findings of Ritala et al. (2020), organizational innovativeness can include five key dimensions: market innovativeness, behavioural innovativeness, process innovativeness, product innovativeness and strategic innovativeness. Product innovativeness is something that is linked with the novelty of products. In addition to this, market innovativeness is linked with the use of new methods, generally with respect to marketing strategies followed by an organization. Besides this, market innovativeness refers to new methods, generally with respect to marketing strategies followed by an organization, in order to get entrance into a particular market. Another dimension of organizational innovativeness is process innovativeness, which depicts a process followed to invent a new product and also the outcome of such a process with the help of new methods or systems used to do work. In addition to this, behavioural innovativeness is linked with change in the conduct of key members of a firm which can help in facilitating the development and adoption of new ideas or processes (Holtgrave et al., 2019).

Organizational Culture and Organizational Innovativeness

Organizational culture is one of the key factors which can help in creating an innovative trend within a firm. It is important for organizations to focus on fulfilling some key necessities for influencing interior behaviours as well as the outside interface in order to adopt technological innovation. The organizational culture is something that can play a role in stimulating individuals' creativity, which can ultimately prove to be helpful in bringing innovativeness within the firm (Quandt and Castilho, 2017). Similar to this, it claimed that in order to enhance innovativeness in an organization, it is highly important to ensure maximum contribution from stakeholders and hence needs a conception of participatory management. On the other hand, Leal-Rodriguez (2020) argued that when there is a specific gap in a position of the market, then this helps in facilitating the awareness of strategic innovation and for taking benefit of it. Moreover, they also claimed that the key focus of organizational innovativeness is on evaluating and developing competencies of a company for the purpose of overcoming key goals of an organization.

In addition to this, Quandt and Castilho (2017) found that behavioural innovativeness in an organization is resulted from creating an innovative culture. The presence of innovative culture works as a vehicle for innovation in an organization. Organizational innovation is basically a radical change in business operations, and it includes the implementation of those changes, which can help in gaining a competitive edge and creating value. Similar to this, Shanker et al. (2017) claimed that the key focus of organizational innovativeness is on searching for ways in order to ensure the fulfilment of organizational goals through effectively utilizing resources. When the culture of an organization is built in such a way that entrepreneurial team characteristics are focused properly, then this ultimately helps in enhancing organizational innovativeness.

Based on a critical review of the literature, it has been found that previously none of the prior research studies investigated the indirect relationship between organizational culture and organizational innovativeness in the context of the Turkish sports sector. So, the current research study is focused on filling this gap.

Moderating Effect of Power Bases

There are five key sources of managerial power, as identified by French and Raven (1959). These sources of managerial power influence the organization in different ways.

Legitimate Power

It is actually a formal power as well as the authority which is legitimately given to the manager, as in accordance with the charter by peers of an organization. The managers in an organization get legitimate power through the written or verbal contract, and it also includes complete detail of the key responsibilities of a manager (French and Raven, 1959). After having this type of power, the manager gets the right direction to employee behaviour, so this sometimes results in reducing the level of creativity and innovativeness among employees. When a completely formal culture is adopted in an organization, then this undermines employees' ability to share creative ideas (Schönberner et al., 2020). However, the research study by Oiliveira and Fraga (2011) identified that the legitimate power hardly affects the organizational cultures for bringing information technology-based adoption models for the organizations.

Reward Power

Reward power is defined as the manager's ability to conferring or withholding the rewards, such as privileges, promotions, financial incentives, and status. This type of power is mostly in use, as, for instance, it is mostly utilized when the employees are promised a day-off in place of working a weekend for meeting the deadlines (Garaus et al., 2016). Therefore, the research explored the moderated impacts of reward power on organizational cultures and innovativeness.

Coercive Power

The type of coercive power is explained as the effective use of force for getting employees for following instructions and orders by the power that came from the subordinate's ability for punishing the employees for the non-compliance behaviours. This type of power is usually applied on a regular basis within the organizations. For instance, this power can enable the employee to carry out an order under the fear of losing their jobs and annual incentives (Singh, 2009).

Therefore, there are two types within the Coercion Power, direct and indirect Coercion Powers. Direct coercion is explained as the deliberate threats by the leaders to elicit specific behaviours. In contrast, indirect coercion power is the type in which the threats are perceived by the employees, regardless of whether it is the real threat or not (Hofmann et al., 2017). Hence, the research study aimed to examine the moderating effects of coercion power on organizational culture and innovativeness.

Expert Power

Expert power is analyzed as the perception that is based on the individual's elevated level of knowledge or the specific skills set, which any other organizations do not have such human resources. For instance, the management of any organization has certain employees with unique knowledge and skills sets, which any other organization do not have. Therefore, these employees are enabling the particular organization to gain competitive advantages (Sahadev, 2005). Hence, this research study aimed to explore the expert power within the organizations of the Turkish sports' sector.

Referent Power

Referent Power is explained as the capability of the leaders to influence the subordinates due to the admiration, identification and respect for the particular leader. Moreover, the employees usually refer to their perspectives and opinions about what they actually think about their leaders and try to do the same (Lunenburg, 2012). This type of power is mostly used by the leaders or managers when they develop their status as the role model for followers to get one or more followers for having effective actions. Nevertheless, this type of power is not a formal power that influences the employees. Instead, it is the personal power that is gained by the leaders or managers by their followers or employees. Therefore, this research study focused on exploring the moderating role of referent power on the organizational culture and innovativeness within the context of the Turkish sports` sector.

Materials and Methods
Research Design

Since the aim of the research study is to examine the impact of organizational culture on organizational innovativeness. For this purpose, the researcher conducted the primary qualitative research study. The survey questionnaire is developed for collecting insightful information from the workers employed within the organizations of the Turkish sports' sector. The reason for selecting this methodology is because it allowed the researcher to interact with the employees and collecting data based on their perceptions. In order to measure organizational culture, the scale developed by Patel et al. (2013), organizational innovativeness by Wang and Ahmet (2004) and organizational power by Hinkin and Schriesheim (1989) has been used.

Population and Sampling

In the data collection method, the study collected the data from 331 employees, of which 77.4% (257 respondents) are male, and 22.3% (74 respondents) are female. Therefore, the collected data from the respondents provided insightful results for identifying the impacts of organizational culture on the organizational innovativeness within the organizations of the Turkish Sport's sector.

Data Analysis

In this research independent variable is organizational innovativeness, and the dependent variable is organizational culture. Similarly, based on the organizational power base, five different moderating variables are involved in the research study, including Legitimate Power, Expert Power, Referent Power, Reward Power, and Coercive Power. For data analysis, the study utilized the SPSS statistical tool for testing the developed hypotheses. For this purpose, the researcher used the statistical tool of Moderated Multiple Regression Model for having insightful results. Moreover, the study also examined the relationship between the variables through the Correlation analysis for examining the strength of the relationship between them. Therefore, the predictive analysis helped in testing the hypothesis of the research study.

Ethical Considerations

The study considered the ethical factors while collecting the primary data, in which the researcher ensured that there is no biasness while collecting the primary data. For this purpose, the researcher ensured that no respondent is forced for taking part in the survey.

Results

This section had analyzed the collected data and provided insightful information for concluding the findings of the research study. Additionally, this section had also discussed the findings with the reviewed literature for concluding the most authentic findings of the study.

Correlation Analysis

The correlation analysis is conducted for examining the strength of the relationship between the variables. Table 1 explains the correlation analysis of examined variables.

Table 1. Correlation Analysis

		Zscore (OC_MEAN)	Zscore (OI_MEAN)	M1	M2	M3	M4	M5
Zscore(OC_MEAN)	Pearson Correlation	1						
Zscore(OI_MEAN)	Pearson Correlation	.680**	1					
M1 (Legitimate P)	Pearson Correlation	-.177**	-.153**	1				
M2 (Expert P)	Pearson Correlation	-.206**	-.379**	.600**	1			
M3 (Referent P)	Pearson Correlation	-.094	-.084	.136*	.194**	1		
M4 (Reward P)	Pearson Correlation	-.033	-.052	.114*	.150**	.143**	1	
M5 (Coercive P)	Pearson Correlation	-.046	-.081	.123*	.180**	.292**	.669**	1

**. Correlation is significant at the 0.01 level (2-tailed).
*. Correlation is significant at the 0.05 level (2-tailed).

The analysis from the correlation analysis shows that moderating variables including Legitimate Power, Expert Power, Referent Power, Reward Power, and Coercive Power have a negative and weak relationship with the independent factor of organizational culture as well as with the dependent variable of organizational innovativeness. However, there is a strong and positive relationship between organizational cultures and organizational innovativeness. Similarly, most of the moderating variables, such as Referent Power, Reward Power, and Coercive Power, have a positive and strong relationship between them. Therefore, it is identified that there is a weak and negative relationship between the moderating and dependent variable.

Moderated Multiple Linear Regression Analysis

Since the research study involved five moderating variables, including Legitimate Power, Expert Power, Referent Power, Reward Power and Coercive Power for data analysis; therefore, the Moderated Multiple Linear Regression analysis is conducted through the SPSS statistics as shown in table 2. The analysis showed that the organizational cultures (independent variable) had a significant impact ($p<0.05$) on the organizational innovativeness (dependent variable) with an 87% change in the slope. Hence the developed hypothesis is tested successfully, which is;

Similarly, reward powers and coercive powers had also no significant impact ($p>0.05$) on organizational innovativeness. Nevertheless, Expert power and Referent power had a significant impact ($p<0.05$) on the organizational innovativeness with the change in the slope for -21% and 1.3% subsequently. Therefore, the analysis showed that there is a moderating effect of expert power and referent power on the relationship between organizational culture and organizational innovativeness.

Table 2. Moderated Multiple Regression Model (*Main Effects*)

	Model 1			Model 2			Model 3		
	B	SE	β	B	SE	β	B	SE	β
(Constant)	.801	.171	.000	.842	.178	0.00	.998	.166	.000
OC (Interaction Variable (IV))	.8760	.052	.000						
IV*M1				-.019	.023	.406			
IV*M2							-.214	.029	.000
IV*M3									
IV-M4									
IV*M5									
ΔR^2 (*Main Effects*)		.680			.681			.736	

	Model 4			Model 5			Model 6		
	B	SE	β	B	SE	β	B	SE	β
(Constant)	.994	.167	.000	.994	.167	.000	.993	.167	.000
OC (Interaction Variable (IV))									
IV*M1									
IV*M2									
IV*M3	.013	.024	.000						
IV-M4				.000	.026	.992			
IV*M5							-.020	.036	.589
ΔR^2 (*Main Effects*)		.736			.736			.736	

Discussion

Based on the statistical analysis, it is identified that there are significant impacts of organizational culture on organizational effectiveness. Similarly, various research studies such as Leal-Rodriguez (2020) and Quandt and Castilho (2017) also identified similar results as the studies identified that the organizational culture could play a significant role in stimulating individuals' creativity which can ultimately prove to be helpful in bringing organizational innovativeness. Moreover, Schönberner et al. (2020) identified that legitimate power could provide a completely formal culture within an organization which could undermine the employees' ability to share creative ideas. Nevertheless, the findings of

Oiliveira and Fraga (2011) argued that there is a weak influence of legitimate power on developing organizational innovativeness based on the employees' behaviours, which is because the legitimacy power emphasizes the formal structures and policies. Similarly, the findings of the research also identified similar results as it is identified that there is no significant moderating effect of legitimate power on the relationship between organizational culture and organizational innovativeness. Hence, contrary to the discussed literature, the findings showed that there is no moderating effect of legitimate power for influencing the role of organizational culture on organizational innovativeness.

Similarly, it is identified in previous literature, such as Hofmann et al. (2017), that reward and coercive powers coexist intrinsically in organizations, due to which the employees are required to balance their perceptions of receiving versus losing. Moreover, Singh (2009) identified that coercive power could enable the employee to carry out an order under the fear of losing their jobs and annual incentives. However, no study identified the significant and moderating impact of reward and coercive powers on the relationship between organizational culture and innovativeness. Additionally, the findings of the research also identified that there are no significant impacts of reward and coercive powers on the relationship between organizational culture and organizational innovativeness. Further, the correlation analysis also showed the weak and negative relationship of moderating variables of the study.

Despite the fact, the findings of the study identified that there is a significant impact of Expert power and Referent power on the relationship between the organizational culture and organizational innovativeness. The findings of the study are also aligned with the previous literature, as it is identified by Lunenburg (2012) that referent power is based upon the less powerful person's identification with the manager. Sahadev (2005) identified expert power as the capability of the management for having certain employees with unique knowledge and skills sets, which any other organization do not have, which results in an increase in creativity and innovativeness. However, the correlation analysis showed that there is a weak and negative relationship between the discussed moderating variables. Hence, based on the critical analysis, it is identified that only two moderating variables, including expert power and referent power, had a significant impact on the relationship between organizational cultures and organizational innovativeness.

Conclusion

The research study identified that there was a significant impact of organizational culture on organizational innovativeness. Nevertheless, it was identified that only two organizational power bases, including expert power and referent power, have a significant and positive moderating influence on the relationship between organizational culture and innovativeness. Therefore, based on the analysis of the findings of this research and previous literature, the study had provided various potential recommendations. Firstly, it is recommended for the organizations that they are required to redesign the existing policies and strategies for expert and referent powers in order to develop organizational innovativeness more effectively. Secondly, the organizations should not neglect the other organizational power bases, including legitimate power, reward and coercive powers, which is because the applications of these powers have some influence on structuring the employees' behaviours for bringing the innovation within the organization. Thirdly, the organizations should integrate people management strategies for managing the employees` behaviours. Therefore, it is identified that organizations are required to rethink the organizational power bases, including expert and referent powers, for influencing organizational innovativeness.

Hence, this research study provided insightful information; however, there is a different limitation within the research study. Firstly, the study is based on a primary quantitative research study, and there is also a need to conduct the research study based on the primary qualitative research for collecting data through in-depth interviews. Therefore, future research studies are recommended to use the suggested methodology. Secondly, the sample size of the research is very broad, which included all the organizations from the Turkish sports` sector. Thus, future research studies are suggested to narrow down the sample size by selecting specific organizations within the Turkish sports` sector.

References

Ardi, A., Djati, S.P., Bernarto, I., Sudibjo, N., Yulianeu, A., Nanda, H.A. and Nanda, K.A., 2020. The Relationship Between Digital Transformational Leadership Styles and Knowledge-Based Empowering Interaction for Increasing Organizational Innovativeness. *International Journal of Innovation, Creativity and Change*, 11(3), pp.259-277.

Bankins, S., Denness, B., Kriz, A. and Molloy, C., 2017. Innovation agents in the public sector: Applying champion and promotor theory to explore innovation in the Australian public service. *Australian Journal of Public Administration*, 76(1), pp.122-137.

Erthal, A. and Marques, L., 2018. National culture and organizational culture in lean organizationns: a systematic review. *Production Planning & Control*, 29(8), pp.668-687.

Frega, J.R., Ferraresi, A.A., Quandt, C.O. and Da Veiga, C.P., 2018. Relationships among knowledge management, organizational innovativeness and performance: Covariance-based versus partial least squares structural equation modelling. *Journal of Information & Knowledge Management*, 17(01), p.1850008.

Garaus, C., Furtmüller, G. and Güttel, W.H., 2016. The hidden power of small rewards: The effects of insufficient external rewards on autonomous motivation to learn. *Academy of Management Learning & Education*, 15(1), pp.45-59.

Gemünden, H.G., Lehner, P. and Kock, A., 2018. The project-oriented organizationn and its contribution to innovation. *International Journal of Project Management*, 36(1), pp.147-160.

Hofmann, E., Hartl, B., Gangl, K., Hartner-Tiefenthaler, M. and Kirchler, E., 2017. Authorities' coercive and legitimate power: the impact on cognitions underlying cooperation. *Frontiers in Psychology*, 8, p.5.

Holtgrave, M., Nayir, D.Z., Nienaber, A.M. and Schewe, G., 2019. Knowledge comes, but wisdom lingers! Learning orientation as the decisive factor for translating social capital into organizational innovativeness and performance in Turkey. *European Journal of International Management*, 13(2), pp.127-158.

Hwang, K. and Choi, M., 2017. Effects of innovation-supportive culture and organizational citizenship behaviour on e-government information system security stemming from mimetic isomorphism. *Government Information Quarterly*, 34(2), pp.183-198.

Kraśnicka, T., Głód, W. and Wronka-Pośpiech, M., 2018. Management innovation, pro-innovation organizational culture and enterprise performance: testing the mediation effect. *Review of managerial science*, 12(3), pp.737-769.

Leal-Rodriguez, A.L., 2020. Generating customer value through the boosting of relationships and organizational innovativeness. *Knowledge Management Research & Practice*, 18(3), pp.336-347.

Lokuge, S., Sedera, D., Grover, V. and Dongming, X., 2019. Organizational readiness for digital innovation: Development and empirical calibration of a construct. *Information & Management*, 56(3), pp.445-461.

Lunenburg, FC, 2012. Power and leadership: An influence process. *International Journal of Management, Business, and Administration*, 15(1), pp.1-9.

Oliveira, T. and Fraga, M., 2011. Literature review of information technology adoption models at firm level.

Patel, P. C., Messersmith, J. G., & Lepak, D. P., 2013. Walking the Tightrope: An Assessment of the Relationship between High-Performance Work Systems and Organizational Ambidexterity. *Academy of Management Journal*, 56(5), pp. 1420-1442.

Quandt, C.O. and Castilho, M.F.D., 2017. Relationship between collaboration and innovativeness: a case study in an innovative organizationn. *International Journal of Innovation and Learning*, 21(3), pp.257-273.

Ritala, P., Vanhala, M. and Järveläinen, K., 2020. The Role Of Employee Incentives And Motivation On Organizational Innovativeness In Different Organizational Cultures. *International Journal of Innovation Management*, 24(04), p.2050075.

Sahadev, S., 2005. Exploring the role of expert power in channel management: An empirical study. Industrial *Marketing Management*, 34(5), pp.487-494.

Schönberner, J., Woratschek, H. and Buser, M., 2020. Understanding sports sponsorship decision-making–an exploration of the roles and power bases in the sponsors' buying centre. *European Sport Management Quarterly*, pp.1-20.

Shanker, R., Bhanugopan, R., Van der Heijden, B.I. and Farrell, M., 2017. Organizational climate for innovation and organizational performance: The mediating effect of innovative work behaviour. *Journal of Vocational Behaviour*, 100, pp.67-77.

Singh, A., 2009. Organizational power in perspective. *Leadership and Management in Engineering*, 9(4), pp.165-176.

Taştan, S.B. and Davoudi, S.M.M., 2017. The relationship between organizational climate and organizational innovativeness: testing the moderating effect of individual values of power and achievement. *International Journal of Business Innovation and Research*, 12(4), pp.465-483.

THE THEORY OF IDEALISM: THE ROAD TO UNDERSTANDING AND EVALUATING IT THROUGH A COMPARISON WITH REALISM

*Ayşe Nur KANLI**

Introduction

The "Thirty Years War" has a crucial place in the formation of the concept of international relations. The war resulted with the peace treaties of Westphalia and led to the separation of religion and politics in which the seeds of secularisation were planted (Şerban, 2013, p. 53). Thus, independent political entities signified the emergence of modern states and the advent of modern states implied the beginning of the practice of international relations. With respect to this, many concepts were developed such as international law, foreign policy, balance of power and so on. However, International Relations (IR) became a separate field of study after the First World War, and an autonomous discipline in the period following the Second World War (Ateş, 2009, p. 11). The behaviour of states and the causes of war became the main topics of debate throughout the two world wars. These debates formed the basis of IR and paved the way for the discipline's first ever theories.

Theories are needed for analysing certain events from a systematic perspective as they offer a clear framework for the researcher. Thus, similar to other disciplines, in order to define, explain and understand international relations IR gave birth to many theories

---

* Istanbul 29 Mayıs University, Faculty of Economics and Administrative Sciences, Political Science and International Relations, Istanbul, Turkey, ORCID Code: https://orcid.org/0000-0002-6995-8976.

(Gözen, 2019, p. 15). From idealism to structuralism, IR has witnessed the emergence of many of them. The development of many theories inevitably induces debate and competition, and such debates help to shape and improve disciplines as well as lead to the enrichment of literature. For instance, the idealism – realism debate has not only established the terminology of the discipline (IR) but also has drawn the boundaries of it (Çalış and Özlük, 2007, p. 226). Therefore, it can be said that the idealism – realism debate has contributed to the formation of IR; however, the crucial role idealism played in the midst of this cannot be ignored.

The contribution of idealist thought to the separation of IR from political science should not be overlooked. While political science has determined its field of study as the state, IR mainly focused on trans-state relations. This is due to the havoc that the First World War had wrecked upon nations. After the war, many people pondered upon the reason behind the cause of it and what could be done in order to prevent another disastrous conflict. The conclusion was the lack of international mechanisms that prevented international conflicts and the existence of authoritarian regimes (Uğrasız, 2003, p. 141). Thus, the promotion of democracy, open diplomacy, establishment of international organisations, and strengthening of international law were put forward as feasible solutions. All these were the outcome of idealist thinking; hence, it can be viewed as the main actor for shaping IR.

However, despite its noteworthy contribution to IR idealism, compared with other theories, is usually left behind when conducting a case study. The reason behind its "unattractiveness" and whether it is a truly competent theory is a matter of ambiguity which this paper will try to explian. The topic of this study is to analyse the theory of idealism and its comparison with realism. The aim of it is to provide an answer to certain questions; such as, what is the importance of idealism in international relations, and why has it failed to achieve recognition within the academia. The scope has been limited to the period of the First World War and the Second World War, with a particular focus on the ideas of important figures. Not only is the paper based on a literature review but also has been prepared under the guidance of the qualitative research method. Lastly, it has been concluded with certain recommendations through the evaluation of the findings that have been acquired. Thus, the following section will explain idealism with its main principles and then compare it with realism which is a frequently used theory that has come to dominate everyday politics.

Understanding Idealism

Idealism is the label that is commonly attached to "utopian and wishful thinking" people and is generally used as a derogatory term (Long, 1991, p. 286). This label was given by E. H. Carr during his battle with British thinkers of International Relations. According to Carr, these scholars were "idealists" due to the fact that they completely ignored the concept of power in the practice of international relations. Moreover, he stated that having a normative agenda would act as a hindrance for a proper analysis regarding the 'real world'. This normative agenda observed by Carr was the desire to establish a peaceful world order in which leaders and policy makers would no longer extol the concept of balance of power (Mearsheimer, 2005, p. 140). However, it is important to note that there is more to this concept than meets the eye as it has a crucial place in the realm of IR and cannot be confined to "utopic" thinking.

The birth of IR as an academic discipline was the outcome of intellectual debates that took place in the aftermath of the First World War. The war had major catastrophic consequences for humanity no doubt; however, it had completely altered the international system. Thus, the reasons behind these debates can be attributed to the desire to restore the peace/bring stability and what could be done in order to prevent another war from happening. Many ideas and solutions were put forward; such as, the need for democracy and democratic institutions, international law and open diplomacy. These formed the basis for idealism as it claimed that the ideas mentioned in the previous sentence had the potential to establish a peaceful system, and ease the mistrust and hostility among states. The most prominent thinker who contributed to this process was President Woodrow Wilson.

Even though the roots of idealist thought can be traced back to Hugo Grotius and contain the theoretical inputs of Immanuel Kant, John Locke, Jean-Jacques Rousseau, Voltaire, and Norman Angell the political input of Woodrow Wilson cannot be ignored. His perception shaped idealism which in return influenced the development of IR. Wilson, pondered upon the possibility of creating a stable and safe international system. Therefore, his main objective was to establish a liberal and democratic world that would be connected through the means of free trade and international law (Çalış and Özlük, 2007, p. 228). He explained his arguments in his famous 14 principles/points. The freedom of movement in the high seas, free trade, open diplomacy, self-determination, the establishment of an international organisation, and disarmament are the few examples regarding his points.

The president further argued and emphasised the organisation of an "open" and "democratic" international system within the framework of a new international institutionalised structure. He believed this could be realised in the establishment of the League of Nations. According to Wilson, the League would be based on a new understanding of collective security; thus, eradicating the outdated balance of power approaches and creating a system based on peace (Uğrasız, 2003, p. 142). With respect to this, an international community would be established and wars would be prevented. Therefore, it can be said that the idealist stance of Woodrow Wilson contributed to the idea of the process of international institutionalisation. This, inevitably, led the activities aiming to form an international society and the rejecting of the "nation-state" structure to gain speed. In addition, Wilson advocated that human beings were inherently good and rational. This argument can be found in the main principles of idealism. Hence, in order to have a better understanding of idealism it is best to explain its basic tenets.

The fundamental assumptions of idealism can be summed up as follows: *Humans are inherently good and rational* (Gözen, 2019). According to this, people have an altruistic impulse and are naturally inclined to act in a good manner. Therefore, mankind cannot be defined as evil spirited. The evil deeds of human beings' stem from the conditions that force people to act as pragmatic tools in order to maximise their interests. Individuals are innately open to cooperation and amicability. Thus, it can be said that if states are governed by such people, it is possible to achieve a permanent peaceful international order.

Cooperation is possible and international anarchy and conflict can be prevented (Gözen, 2019). Idealists believe that an important way to prevent conflict is giving the public the opportunity to express itself which can only be done in a democracy. The expansion of democratic regimes would make it less likely for states to go to war. This is due to the fact that democratic governance is the manifestation of the "general will". It upholds the rule of law and respects the rights and freedoms of people. Thus, the increasing number of such regimes and their shared values would avert a possible confrontation (the famous dictum "democracies don't fight each other) (Viotti and Kauppi, 2012, p. 154). Furthermore, democracies are expected to prioritise the common good rather than the national interest and engage in cooperation in order to ensure the former.

International organisations contribute to the international order (Gözen, 2019). Idealists do not reject the state as they accept it to be the main actor in international relations. However, they also acknowledge the presence of international organisations and their effect on the international system. These organisations not only act as an arena for solving disputes but also increase the web of interconnectedness between states. Nations come to rely on each other (interdependence) in this complex web of ties and the cost of breaking them starts to outweigh the benefits. Therefore, international organisations help to ensure the stability of the international order.

Progress is possible (Gözen, 2019). The nature of human beings, the harmony of interest between states, the effort for improving human life and the prioritisation of the common good leads to progress. Idealists believe that advancements in certain aspects of life will result in an improved state of human condition. It is also associated with the concept of modernisation.

Pluralism, interdependence, globalisation, and the importance of both high and low politics may also be added to the list. Of course, idealism is not just the sum of these assumptions but also is composed of crucial concepts and themes. Even though idealism and liberalism differ from each other they share common features and notions; for instance, collective security, integration, functionalism and the spill-over effect, positive-sum calculations, absolute gains, international regimes, and change. These assumptions and concepts more or less form the basis of idealism. Though the theory of idealism seems quite adequate and has the potential to meet the demands of International Relations it lost its appeal when the League of Nations failed to prevent the Second World War. The decline of idealism led to the rise of another theory which, hitherto, dominates the academia and today's politics: realism.

Realism vs. Idealism: The Tale of an Epic Battle

After the Second World War, realism entered the literature of international politics as a mainstream theory (Babahanoğlu and Bilici, 2018, p. 735). According to the classical understanding of realism, international relations is the struggle for power. Thus, the primary objective of any state is to maximise its own power and prioritise its security. The concept of "security dilemma" has a central place in realism as it leads a state to believe that others are continuously trying to gain power at its expense and seek its destruction. Idealism, on the other hand, does not recognise this concept and deems the problems and policies stemming from it irrational. It rather focuses on "rational conditions or rational solutions" (Wright, 1952, p. 117). Moreover, realists claim that states act in a selfish manner and pursue their national interest while idealists reject this notion and state the importance of common good and cooperation.

Contrary to idealism, realism puts forward the idea that human beings are inherently bad and are imbued with the need to dominate and exploit. In addition, due to the fact that "values" are often associated with idealism, realists stray away from this and insist that power is the ultimate value for states to pursue. For instance, Wright (1952) claimed the following:

> ...Thus, when it is said that states pursue power as their supreme value, the philosophical question is at once raised: Ought power to be the supreme value of states? The "realist" answers affirmatively, asserting that states should pursue their national interests and the supreme national interest is the augmentation of the state's power position. They are, however, then asserting not a self-evident axiom but an ethical norm, and an ethical norm which is by no means uncontroversial. Can it be said that the Alexanders, Caesars, Napoleons, and Hitlers who appeared to make power their goal are better examples of statesmanship than the Washingtons, Jeffersons, Lincolns, and Wilsons who appeared to subordinate power to other values? (p. 122)

Furthermore, because realists view the international arena as the struggle for power, they give little attention to international law and organisations. Hence, unlike idealists who believe in the harmony of interests, realists have a negative stance towards the possibility of cooperation as they emphasise that reality is composed of conflict of interests. Regarding international law, realism is rather sceptical due to the belief that it acts as a tool and serves the powerful. The concept of balance of power is offered as a means to ensuring stability. They further believe that the chief obligation of the state is not towards an ambiguous international community but rather to its own citizens. Realists criticise idealists for proposing disarmament, logic, and goodwill as the solution to preventing wars (Uğrasız, 2003, p. 144). Accordingly, such a solution is rather impractical/useless as it ignores the "realities" of world politics which is the inevitability of war.

Therefore, it can be said that the obsoleteness of international law, the absence of a higher authority, the struggle for power, the supreme position of the nation-state, and the perpetual conflict among states make up the anarchical structure of the international system. Realists put forward that international anarchy cannot be prevented and counter attack Kant's arguments by asserting the views of Machiavelli (*ends justify the means*) and Hobbes (*man is a wolf to man*). Thus, realists have often labelled idealists as utopian thinkers for ignoring the *Realpolitik* character of international politics. Today, it is possible to observe that realists have contributed much to the literature of politics. For instance, hegemony, balance of power, status quo, deterrence, anarchy are few of the many concepts formulated by them. Realism has been accepted as a problem-solving theory in which it propels statesmen to take the world as it is and navigate accordingly. Contrary to the normative character of idealism, realism has advocated the importance of positivism in theory making.

In sum, idealists claim that it is possible to organise a peaceful international system in accordance with cooperation, international organisations, international law, justice, and disarmament rather than just accepting world politics as it is. On the other hand, realists claim that struggle, power, and interest form the basis of the reality of politics and thus states should rely on no other but themselves. Idealism, though accepts states as important actors, focuses on humanity and thus has a holistic perspective while realism focuses only on states and hence has a state-centric approach. With respect to this, realist thinkers have accused idealists for not being parsimonious enough. The former maintained that trying to include every actor and aspect in international relations would only breed confusion. All of these may be considered as the reason behind "the state of unattractiveness" of idealism.

In addition to the previous paragraph, it can also be observed that today's world is composed of proxy wars, economic wars, and the struggle to exist/survive. Therefore, in such a world it is most natural for realism to dominate the language of politics and for idealism to be left behind. However, due to this, many scholars overlook the contribution and importance of idealist projects, norms and values; to exemplify, the European Union can be considered as the actualisation of idealism. Furthermore, it is important to note that idealism is acknowledged as long as it sustains/maintains these values. It is bound for failure if it completely ignores the reality of power. The same argument can be applied to realism in which the lack of attention given to values result in the understanding that life is nothing more than a zero-sum game. Thus, as it can be seen "no single approach can capture all the complexity of contemporary world politics" (Walt, 1998, p. 30).

Conclusion

To conclude, though the practice of international relations can be traced back to the Peace of Westphalia (1648) it was not until the outbreak of the First World War that it made its appearance as a separate discipline. The birth of International Relations led to the emergence of many theories that tried to analyse world politics in a systematic way. The most important of these theories is idealism; due to the fact that, it contributed to the shaping of the discipline and established the first great debate. The philosophical roots of idealism can be found in early modern history; however, it would gain its political dimension with the input of Woodrow Wilson. Idealism, in short, believes that humans are inherently good, cooperation is possible, international organisations can be helpful, international anarchy can be prevented, and international law has the potential to ensure peace and stability. However, idealism entered into a period of decline after its ideas proved to be a failure with the outbreak of the Second World War.

The decline of idealism led to the rise of realism. This school of thought was the complete opposite of idealist thought. It claimed the "real world" was nothing more than a naked struggle for power within the international anarchy where the security dilemma prevailed. Anything other than the state was accepted as rather irrelevant and few concepts were brought forward; such as, the balance of power and hegemony. Due to the current situation of world politics many statesmen and thinkers prefer to utilise the principles of realism. Due to this, the valuable teachings of idealism are often ignored. However, it should not be forgotten that the view that realism paints is rather bleak. I believe that adopting a realist mindset is nothing more than choosing the easy path for conducting political affairs. The system in which people operate in has been created by no other but themselves and thus it is the belief of the people that has the power to reconstruct it according to idealist principles. Of course, claiming that idealism is the pinnacle of theories would be a wrong approach as both theories have their shortcomings. Thus, no theory has the potential to capture every aspect of international relations. What could be done is to harmonise both theories as they both have complementary forces and develop a new one which gives importance to relevant concepts that are not detrimental to the welfare of humanity.

References

Ateş D 2009. Uluslararası ilişkiler disiplinin oluşumu: İdealizm/Realizm tartışması ve disiplinin özerkliği. Doğuş Üniversitesi Dergisi, 10(1): 11-25.

Babahanoğlu V, Bilici Z 2018. Realizm versus idealizm: Göç, bölgesel barış ve istikrar düşmanı mı? Uluslararası Sosyal Araştırmalar Dergisi, 11(61): 734-740.

Çalış Ş, Özlük E 2007. Uluslararası ilişkiler tarihinin yapısökümü: İdealizm-Realizm tartışması. Selçuk Üniversitesi Sosyal Bilimler Enstitüsü Dergisi, 18: 225-243.

Gözen R 2019. İdealizm. In: Gözen R (ed), Uluslararası ilişkiler teorileri. İstanbul: İletişim Yayınları, pp. 67-120.

Long D 1991. J. A. Hobson and idealism in international relations. Review of International Studies, 17(3): 285-304.

Mearsheimer JJ 2005. E. H. Carr vs. idealism: The battle rages on. International Relations, 19(2): 139-152.

Şerban I 2013. Theories and concepts in international relations – From idealism to realism. Revista de Stiinte Politice. Revue des Sciences Politiques, (40): 52-59.

Uğrasız B 2003. Uluslararası ilişkilerde iki farklı yaklaşım: idealizm ve realizm. Dokuz Eylül Üniversitesi Sosyal Bilimler Enstitüsü Dergisi, 5(2): 139-145.

Viotti PR, Kauppi MV 2012. International relations theory. Illinois: Longman.

Walt SM 1998. International relations: one world, many theories. Foreign Policy, 29-46.

Wright Q 1952. Realism and idealism in international relations. World Politics, 5(1): 116-128.

DEVELOPMENT OF STATE BUILDING PROCESS AND THE FORMATION OF A POLITICAL SYSTEM IN THE MIDDLE EAST

*Kaan DİYARBAKIRLIOĞLU**

Introduction

We witness important events in the historical process in the Middle East region, which is located in a wide geography. It is important to consider the much longer development context in this large region, not even ten-year trends, but at least those that have emerged over the last century. Under the Sykes-Pico agreement, Levant and Mesopotamia were divided by Great Britain and France in such a way that the ethnic and cultural lines and the newly formed political boundary lines became a structure where peace could never come again. According to Alexei Simakov: "The states designed as Iraq and Syria, likewise Libya, Yemen and many more around the world, were neither large enough to force co-existence upon their many ethno-linguistic groups, as the Ottoman Empire did, nor with a common enough historical identity to form a cohesive society, as is Oman."[1]

Over the course of a hundred-year development, a close interweaving of trends of various levels has been revealed, affecting the state of affairs with varying degrees of intensity and uneven tem-

---

* Yalova University, Faculty of Economics and Administrative Sciences, ORCID ID: 0000-0003-4511-5330.
[1] Alexei Simakov, "The Tragedy of Colonial Borders", *The McGill International Review*, Nov. 4, 2015, at https://www.mironline.ca/the-tragedy-of-colonial-borders, accessed on June 13, 2020.

poral depth. The most important of them can be combined into several clusters: global and regional factors, as well as long-term, medium-term and short-term regional trends. In the literature of international relations, some of them that have had the most significant impact on Middle East reality can be listed. These are the formation of statehood and the universalization of political systems, globalization / regionalization of world politics, the changing role of the West in the international arena, the formation of the integrity of the global economic system and the world economic specialization of countries and regions, high demographic dynamics, modernization and complication of social structures, increasing the significance of the religious factor in public life and public consciousness, and the rise and decline of major ideological movements.

It is clear that these processes found their concrete, often quite specific manifestation in the Middle East. Some of the featured events are: the region was involved quite tightly; in others, it remained mainly a recipient of external influences. Having come into contact with a peculiar local reality, global factors acquire the character of mega-trends of regional ones. However, the latter were by no means always a derivative of global processes, sometimes they were produced by the local environment and were only indirectly associated with extra-regional reality. Interaction with her could have a conflicting character. The same is with regional long-term, medium-term and short-term trends. They partly became a concrete embodiment of trends developing in a wider context, spatially localized, and partly turned out to be a product and manifestation of specific historical circumstances. In this article, three most important consequences of this dynamic deserve primary attention: Firstly, the question of how it affected the formation and development of political systems in the macro-region. Secondly, how international relations were formed here in the intra-regional space. Finally, how factors of internal development influenced the positioning of the region in relations with the outside world.

The Formation and the Development of the Political Systems in the Region

The twentieth century gave rise to very diverse ways of political organization of society. The spectrum of political systems "tested" over the course of a century seems surprisingly wide, from absolutist monarchical forms and various (including the most severe) variations of totalitarianism to liberal, democratic and social-paternalistic orders. A paradox in this regard may seem to be the idea that the definite universalization of political systems ultimately became the most important global factor of political development in the 20th century. The term "universalization" is probably not ideal, as it needs to be clarified. It means the totality of some parameters that are considered necessary in the political architecture of any state formation, regardless of its genesis, ideology, self-identification and other specific characteristics inherent in it.

Among these parameters there are many such that directly correlate with two concepts - "democratization" and "modernization". It would seem that they should be preferred. But here certain ideological and historical connotations are obvious, which are not always relevant in certain particular circumstances or acceptable to participants in political processes. There is another consideration: although the adoption of some elements of democracy and the corresponding institutions that accompany the transformation of political systems has become widespread, it seems not justified to speak of democratization as the main vector of movement in this area. On the one hand, the phenomenon of democracy itself is quite complex and ambiguous, which comes to light as it emerges and develops. On the other hand, there are many examples of how totalitarian regimes legitimized themselves through formally democratic procedures. Reservations of a similar kind seem to be valid with respect to the widespread concept of modernization: it is clear that it contains the idea of overcoming the socio-political archaic, but does not answer the question of how and in which direction.

The term "universalization" seems to be more cautious and neutral and therefore more appropriate, especially in relation to the macro-region under consideration. Here, the constitution of the political system took place through the formation of the state on the basis of the formation of a national community as its foundation. This process, to a large extent, was going on with the active introduction of Western experience in state building onto the Middle East soil.

States emerging in the Middle East in the twentieth century can be divided into several types[2]. The first of them is the states that emerged as a result of national liberation movements in the place of dependent territories (colonies, protectorates, mandated areas). In this category, I highlight those formations whose peoples in the past (sometimes very old ones) had their own established statehood and only then became dependent on global or regional powers - the Ottoman Empire, Great Britain, France. In most cases, their borders were perceived as historically legitimate. The most striking example of such a state is Egypt, in whose culture the idea of political subjectivity has existed since antiquity, regardless of which empires included this country and how its borders in the south changed. Another example is Morocco, where the Alawite dynasty has invariably ruled since the 17th century. The third type is states that emerged in the place of dependent territories that never possessed their own statehood. Their borders were determined by the mother countries at the beginning of the colonial period, as a rule, arbitrarily, without taking into account the natural-geographical and demographic realities. Such states include Iraq, Syria, and Libya. Kuwait under the Ottoman Empire was part of the Basra province (which subsequently gave rise to Saddam Hussein to consider him part of Iraq), but then became a British protectorate and gained independence only in 1961. The formation of such states was usually not easy. For example, in the case of Libya, which was previously controlled by Italy, the question arose of dividing the country into three independent provinces. Great Britain tried to

---

[2] For another comparison of the types of the states by management styles in the middle east , see Mehran Kamrava, *The modern Middle East : a political history since the First World* War,2nd ed., University of California Press Berkeley and Los Angeles, California, 2011, pp-297-299.

recognize the independent Cyrenaica at the United Nations, while France wanted to get Fezzan under the administration, agreeing to transfer Cyrenaica and Tripolitania to British control. Then the Soviet Union advocated the formation of Libya as a single country, and its position played a role in preventing its division into separate mini-states.

The fourth type is states created on the basis of intra-regional expansion or external construction through the migration process. In the first case, it is Saudi Arabia, in the second - Israel, whose claims on part of Palestine were recognized by international law. Israel, of course, is a unique example of the formation of a modern state. The leaders of the Zionist movement set the task of returning to the land where the kingdom of Israel once existed and from where the Jews were finally expelled by the Romans in 70 CE. In the XIX century, almost eighteen centuries later, Jewish organizations began teaching Hebrew as a national language (and not just a language of worship) in schools. In subsequent periods the active colonization of Palestine, the leaders of Zionism recreated Hebrew as a living national language (neo-Hebrew). Language, therefore, served as an important tool for the formation of a new national identity and social transformation, as was the case in some other situations in the Middle East (among the Arabs in the Ottoman Empire, and then in the colonial era, or among the Turks in the post-Ottoman era). The fifth type is represented by one state. Turkey is an example for this. After the defeat in the First World War, Turkey entered a new stage in its history within the boundaries significantly narrowed compared with the four hundred year imperial era. Of course, this is far from the only example of a state that is the former core of a large regional empire that has lost most of its territories. Phobias and complexes on this basis can have a very long-term character, especially in an unstable international political environment. In Turkey, part of the elite has not overcome the temptation of neo-imperial illusions, which continues to have some influence on state policy in our time. The sixth and final type is Iran, or former Persia. The uniqueness of this country is that for centuries it has maintained the continuity of statehood mainly in historical, albeit changing, borders. Over the past century, the political evolution of the state has been saturated with deep perturbations and transformations. On the way from the Qajar monarchy to a modern state, Iran went through the outbursts of civil war and separatism (Gilan Republic, the Mehabad Republic), the change of dynasty, coup (organized from the outside), the experience of de-Islamization, and finally the 1979 Shiite revolution, which led to the creation of the Islamic republic with its unique combination of elements of theocratic regime and democracy today. Add to this the foreign occupation (twice - in the 20s and 40s) and aggression from Iraq in the 80s of the last century.

The most important element of state building in all six cases was political engineering, the essence of which was the attempt to consciously transfer Western norms, principles, standards, and algorithms for the functioning of the political system to local soil. In a number of cases, mainly in protectorates and other dependent territories, this line was drawn by colonial authorities to increase efficiency management, which contributed to the creation of institutions adequate to European (ministries and departments, political parties and movements, etc.). In other situations, the local elites who sought political modernization, including those leading the national liberation struggle, became engineering agents. Finally, there were examples when such engineering was carried out by external forces, forcibly and without taking into account local characteristics.

There is a fairly clear correlation between the borrowing of Western experience in state building and socio-economic modernization. Thus, for the Gulf States, the motive for acquiring modern political institutions was mainly the desire to obtain a "pass" to the world political and economic system. However, as modernization processes developed, the need to adapt traditional legal and political systems to international standards gradually became less formal and more meaningful. When building a modern state, the Middle Eastern elites had to voluntarily or involuntarily tackle, among other things, the solution of the national question.

The problem here was that the political entities that existed in the Middle East, built on their own principles and models of government, did not need the idea of a nation, whether civil or ethnic. Introducing Middle Eastern intellectuals in the 19th - early 20th centuries with the theories of nationalism led to the emergence of relevant concepts in regional debates. The liberation struggle that unfolded after the First World War brought the discussion that had already begun into practice, as a result of which three main approaches to nation-building appeared in the Arab world.

The first (Pan-Arab) was based on the idea of linguistic and ethnic unity in the spirit of 19th century German nationalism. The second (country-based) approach had several variations. In some countries, it was historically and geographically determined and in one form or another in some countries, it was historically and geographically determined in either existed in a different form before in Egypt. In others, it was formed during the struggle for independence in Tunisia and Algeria. In the second, it appeared after the proclamation of statehood in Sudan, Libya, and in the monarchy of the Gulf. Finally, the third approach can be defined as Islamic. It was a purely Middle Eastern invention and involved a conversion of ideas *Umma* (the entire Muslim community connected by Islamic ties) into the idea of a nation.

Over the course of a hundred years of the development of the region, none of these three approaches has been able to supplant the others, as a result of which discussions about the nation, national unity, community or difference of courts have always remained the most important element of social life. However, the nation-building process was one of the central for non-Arab states of the region. However, the nation-building process was one of the central for non-Arab states of the region.

If in Turkey the principle of a nation-state was immediately adopted by the Kemalist[3] elite and only by the end of the last century began to be supplemented with the ideas of pan-Turkism and

---

[3] See Ayşe Kadioğlu, "The paradox of Turkish nationalism and the construction of official identity", *Middle Eastern Studies* (32) 2, 1996, pp, 1188-189.

neo-Ottomanism[4], then in Iran and Israel the situation was more complicated. The founding fathers of Israel thought their creation was the embodiment of the age, old dream of the Jewish people, and ethnic and religious identities were the cornerstones of the new statehood. In Iran, the same role was played by the Farsi language, the idea of a common imperial past and the belonging of the majority of the population to Shiism.

Finally, in the region there are at least two peoples who have formed a developed national identity over the past century, but without statehood. These are Kurds and Palestinian Arabs. The Kurds established an autonomous regional administration in Northern Iraq. Palestine is divided into two parts, the West Bank and Gaza, which, de facto, do not have connection each other.

On the whole, it can be stated that state building in the region throughout the last century has developed with the preservation of significant institutional imbalances. The process of establishing national integrity in no country in the region went according to the European model and was not completed. This gave rise to the well-known hybridity of Middle Eastern statehood and gives reason to believe that the formation of nation-states in the Middle East can only be discussed with a certain degree of conditionality. Powerful tribal institutions and ethno-confessional community perfectly adapted to this unbalanced and often unstable institutional reality, sometimes filling it with completely unexpected content. Not only did they not unravel the conflict nodes in society, but, on the contrary, they often strengthened the lines of opposition, and sometimes gave new forms to old conflicts. The deeply rooted traditions of authoritarianism, together with the initial weakness of the institutions of representation, predetermined the monopolization of power by "strong personalities". As a result of the process, state building took on a clearly personified character.

All these circumstances gave rise to accusations of the Middle East countries in rejection of modernization. They don't see the

---

[4] Yilmaz Çolak, "Ottomanism vs. Kemalism: Collective memory and cultural pluralism in 1990s Turkey", *Middle Eastern Studies*, (42) 4, 2006, p. 588.

state building efforts as a result of their own creative development, but an instrument of oppression. The process of modernization in the Middle East acquired a specific character and developed through the formation of hybrid political systems. They sometimes turned out to be a little balanced, which in many states became the source of the formation of permanent socio-political tension and a high level of political violence.

All Middle East states that have become independent have achieved independence due to the broad-based liberation movement. It arose and gained strength as a result of the rapid growth of national self-consciousness, which forced the mother country to grant independence to the peoples of these countries. Although almost all of them went through a series of uprisings, mass demonstrations, strikes and other large-scale protest actions, independence in the final analysis in most cases took place peacefully. The exception is two countries (Algeria, 1962 and South Yemen, 1967) where independence was gained during the armed struggle.

In conclusion, the universalization of political systems as a global mega-trend at the regional level corresponded state and nation-building that begins at the final stage of the First World War and continues until the late 1950s and early 1960s, when most countries in the region became independent. In the 60s of the twentieth century, the region entered the next phase of its development, when the radical transformation of a number of states began and at the same time the accumulation of combustible material, which ultimately led to a powerful explosion in the form of an "Arab awakening".

Intra-Regional Relations

Over the past hundred years, several fundamental transformations have occurred in the system of international relations. With all the diversity of factors of the global plan, they can be reduced to globalization, which had three main dimensions. First, a unified world political system is emerging and evolving within the framework of the Versailles-Washington, and then the Yalta-Potsdam world order. It is a political dimension of globalization. As this system developed, the role of all its main participants changed - primarily the West, but also Russia (the Soviet Union). Their mutual confrontation evolved from a tough confrontation to cooperative interaction algorithms. Allied relations during the Second World War, peaceful coexistence, and détente were the examples of that. The unconditional dependence of vassals on the "grands" of world politics in place of colonialism has been replaced by more flexible forms of domination. After the end of the bipolar international system, contours of a unipolar world arise, but they are increasingly being replaced by a tendency to form a polycentric international system. As this development occurs, the character and imperatives of leadership in the international political arena change. Secondly, the formation of a global economy takes place. On the other hand, the specialization of individual economies is being formed and gains momentum within the global system. For them, this is a condition of competitiveness and survival, and for the world economy, it is a factor of sustainability and an effective response to emerging challenges and stresses. Thirdly, and finally, a single global intellectual-value space is gradually developing. It is developing unevenly in different country and regional spaces, sometimes with a noticeable lag behind economic and political globalization, but, which is very noteworthy, with quite tangible consequences for both.

The signs of this process are the gradual formation of universal ideas about the values and meanings of social development, the emergence of globalist motives in ideological discourses, the universalization of cultural stereotypes. In this area, more than in any other, a sharply increased role of the media factor, in general, mass communication media, propaganda and manipulative capacity is revealed.

Let us now consider all these processes at the regional Middle East level. The process of integration of the Middle East into the emerging world political system began as early as the 19th century. However, almost all of them were included in it initially as colonially dependent territories and were not considered as components of a single regional space with their own subjectivity.

Actually, before the end of World War I, it can be talked about the existence of four separate regions, or "worlds" in the place of the modern Middle East, each of which developed more or less in its own logic. First of the four region is the "Ottoman world" concentrated around the centers of the Ottoman Empire, which included the space from Turkey (in the north) to Iraq (in the east), then to Jordan and Hejaz (part of the future Saudi Arabia) (in the south) and finally to Egypt (at the southwestern tip of the described territorial range). Second one is basically the "Iranian world", limited by the territory of Persia, which extended its influence to the South Caucasus and partly to Central Asia. Third is the "Arabian world", to some extent oriented towards the Indian Ocean, but on the whole rather closed on it. Finally, the fourth region is the 'Mediterranean world', which included the Maghreb countries. Despite the fact that all four worlds belonged to a common historical, cultural, and religious space, they were politically and economically little connected with each other. In this regard, it is noteworthy that the early Pan-Arab projects put forward at the beginning of the twentieth century did not extend to the Maghreb countries. The formation of the Versailles-Washington system and the emergence of a project of a Jewish national center in Palestine, however, contributed to the gradual formation of a common regional identity, especially in the Arab countries. Possessing linguistic, religious, and historical-cultural unity, they occupied an approximately equally dependent position in the formed system of international relations and early felt the injustice of this system. It also affected that, one way or another, it supported the Zionist movement. Turkey and Iran were initially perceived as external to the region of the country. Nevertheless, they gradually turned out to be included in it, which was also associated with a change in the foreign policy of these two countries. Over time these two countries moved away from an exclusive orientation toward the West.

The emergence of regional Middle Eastern identity has become a key factor in the regional factor of the twentieth century. International relations in the region can be considered as a subsystem within the framework of a common system of international relations. This subsystem has its own characteristics. First, the state-building process in many countries of the region occurred during the colonial period. Therefore, global actors have been involved in the internal processes of these countries from the very beginning.

During the colonial period, colonial states such as Britain and France deployed their troops into the region. For this reason, it took a long time for new states to achieve their goals even after gaining independence. The degree of foreign intervention in regional processes has decreased slightly after overcoming colonialism. However, the bipolarity that replaced the colonialism created its own tools to influence the area from the outside. As a result, in the most acute situations that arise, in the "zero-sum game" (as in 1973), posing a serious threat to turn the Middle East into a global conflict factor, the two superpowers USA and the Soviet Union played a decisive role involving the countries of the region. As the Soviet Union aimed to spread communism in the region, the USA tried to prevent it[5]. After 1991, the United States became the main external security partner for the states of the region, having resorted to direct military intervention several times[6]. Its purpose was either to reformat individual segments of the region (2003, Iraq), or, conversely, to prevent such a thing for its interests[7]. However, Russian military intervention to Syria in 2015 to save Bashar al-Assad's regime was a cornerstone in Middle East. Thus, Russia reasserted itself as a major player in the region's power politics. Moscow's bold use of military power positioned it as an important actor in the Middle East[8]. The effect of getting used to the presence of

---

[5] J. F. Jeffrey & M. Eisenstadt, "US military engagement in the broader Middle East," *Policy Focus*, 143, 2016, pp.10-11.
[6] Kenan Dagci, "AB ve ABD'nin Orta Dogu Stratejileri ve Buyuk Orta Dogu Projesi," in A. Sandikli & Kenan Dagci (Eds.), *Buyuk Orta Dogu Projesi*, TASAM, 2006, p. 175.
[7] Kenan Dagci, "ABD'nin Yeni Güvenlik Yaklaşımı ve Terörizm," *Avrasya Dosyası*, 12(s 3), 2006, p.75.
[8] E. Rumer, *Russia in the Middle East: Jack of All Trades, Master of None*, Carnegie Endowment for International Peace, 2019, p.i.

external players in the region and the demand for their active participation in the formation of the security system is noteworthy. For some regional powers, this has become a natural factor in Middle East reality. For example, the Obama administration's desire to reduce US involvement in Middle Eastern affairs and abandon anti-Iranian politics was perceived by the Gulf monarchies as a betrayal[9].

Another feature of the subsystem formed in the Middle East is its exclusivism, the building of regional unity on the basis of the opposition of all countries of the region to one common enemy, who is considered "alien". At first, Israel played the role of such an enemy, and the Arab-Israeli conflict was central an element of regional relations for half a century. Then the enemy for a significant part of the Arab states which are considered as the stronghold of Sunni Islam such as Saudi Arabia was Iran. Thus, a regional factor can be considered the formation of a regional subsystem dependent on external actors with a strong component of the exclusivist confrontation. Moreover, the regional subsystem was always heterogeneous, and its internal structure still retains the memory of the not so distant past. A concrete expression of such a memory was the unification projects at the sub-regional level. There were some political developments in the region at the sub-regional level. However, such initiatives did not achieve the expected success. For example, the League of Arab States was created in 1945, which played a prominent role in resolving disputes between its members, but ultimately failed to become an effective tool for managing regional processes. Another case is that Egypt and Syria merged into one state in 1958 as the United Arab Republic, however, lasted only until September 1961, disintegrating due to sharp contradictions between the elites of the two countries. A similar example, Iraq and Jordan announced the creation of an "Arab Federation" in 1957, which Kuwait was invited to join, but it refused. The anti-monarchist revolution in Iraq prevented the implementation of this project on July 14, 1958.

---

[9] Hérodote, (149) 2, 2013, p. 22 .

The Gulf Cooperation Council (GCC) was established in 1981. GCC is a political and economic alliance. While slowly evolving towards an important integration (a single regional currency, a customs union similar to the Euro etc.), due to the Arab Spring uprisings relations among the members of the GCC have been disrupted. Egypt and GCC members Saudi Arabia, the United Arab Emirates, and Bahrain instated a blockade against Qatar in 2017.

Egypt, Iraq, Jordan, and the Republic of Yemen established the Council for Arab Cooperation, a sub-regional association, in 1989. However, the aggression of Saddam Hussein against Kuwait in 1990 put an end to this organization.

There are other attempts made in the western part of the region to unite the states of North Africa within the framework of the Arab Maghreb Union. But it has not had any activity since 1994. Periodic attempts to revive this structure are mainly related to external impulses from the EU or European countries seeking to unite their southern partners with the aim of promoting Mediterranean cooperation[10]. However, the integration processes in the region have not been seriously developed, and the nation-state in its specific Middle Eastern form has survived as the main form of organization of life in Middle Eastern societies, withstanding many challenges. The failures of the integration projects seem to be related primarily to their lack of economic feasibility. The relative success of the GCC appears to be due to the initially leading role of Saudi Arabia in this organization. Nevertheless, small Gulf state's foreign policy, as they reinforced their economy, became increasingly independent, which led to the accumulation of contradictions among them and Saudi Arabia and hindered the possibility of integration development. In this regard, weakening of sub-regional integration can also be considered as a regional important trend.

Another trend is the conflicts rising over the century in the region. They are directly related to the distinguished features of the

---

[10] Kenan Dagci, "The EU's Middle East Policy and Its Implications to the Region", Alternatives: Turkish Journal of International Relations, Vol. 6, No.1&2, Spring & Summer 2007, pp. 180-183.

Middle East subsystem of intraregional relations. One of the longest and difficult to resolve conflicts is related to the Palestinian problem and the formation of Israel. Several wars broke out between these two people. Moreover, the region survived a large number of other wars, armed clashes, revolutions, counter-revolutions and coups. Both state and non-state actors acted as parties to the conflicts. Conflicts were generated by reasons of a systemic and political nature of the region. The main fundamentals of these reasons include deep contradictions between different ethnic and religious groups, a lack of historical legitimacy of state borders and territorial disputes[11], the relative weakness of all Middle Eastern players, mutual distrust of the elites, etc. and created the basis for endless contest for regional leadership.

Prior to the independence of most countries, major conflicts occurred between the local population and the colonial authorities. Most often, they took on the character of anti-government protests, but sometimes turned into full-fledged civil wars. The formation of Israel caused regional conflicts and instability within the region[12]. Most of the wars are directly or indirectly connected with it until the 1980s. Iran-Iraq war in 1980-1988, which was a long and bloody war in the history of the Middle East, Iraq's occupation of Kuwait in 1990, and the Algerian Civil War (1990-1998)[13]. Finally, already during the "Arab awakening" new conflicts arise in Libya, Syria and Yemen, which are turning into the arena of proxy wars for a number of countries in the region. The reasons for the continuous increase in violence in the Middle East are not main topic of this piece, but they appear to be connected mainly not with international relations, but with the dynamics of development within the region. Therefore, focusing on the some important aspects of this development that affect its positioning in relation to the outside

---

[11] Ahmet Davutoglu, *Stratejik Derinlik*, Kure yayinlari, Istanbul, 2001, p. 323-324.
[12] M. E. Sørli, N. P. Gleditsch & H. Strand, "Why is there so much conflict in the Middle East?, *Journal of Conflict Resolution*, 49(1), 2005, p. 146.
[13] See Luis Martinez, *The Algerian Civil War, 1990-1998*, (Translated from the French by Jonathan Derrick,) C. Hurst and Co.(Publishers) Ltd, 2000.

world is a necessity to understand abovementioned dynamics of interaction with the external world in the region.

Implications of the Internal Developments in Positioning of the Region in Relations with the Outside World

It is clear that decolonization and the formation of independent states encouraged country elites to build their own models of economic development, taking into account the specifics of each country. However, possessing unequal resource such as infrastructure and human potential at the initial stage, the states of the region, nevertheless, took approximately similar positions in the world economy and were forced to solve similar tasks of socio-economic modernization. Over time, the situation has begun to change. Due to the huge needs of the energy sector, powerful incentives arose for the oil and gas industry in a number of countries, which soon removed them from the general number of developing countries and turned them into key suppliers of energy resources. The most important regional factor has become growing differences in the structures of the economies of the states of the region and in the niches occupied by them in the world economy. The result of the rapid economic growth of oil-exporting countries has been the accumulation of their huge amount of financial resources and, accordingly, the acquisition of new opportunities for impact on the external environment. In particular, a considerable part of these funds is spent on military preparations, the activation of which, in turn, can also be considered as one of the trends of the last decades. For instance, US companies, Raytheon, Lockheed Martin, Boeing, and General Dynamics were involved in the majority of arms offers from 2009 through May 2019. In all, the four companies were involved in 27 offers worth over $125 billion, out of a total of 51 offers to Saudi Arabia worth $138 billion[14]. At the same time, the volumes and high quality of armaments and military equipment significantly exceed the needs and capabilities of the Arab monar-

---

[14] See Cassandra Stimpson & William Hartung, *U.S. Arms Sales to Saudi Arabia: The Corporate Connection*, Center For International Policy (Arms and Security Project), July 2019, p.1.

chies of the Gulf, which are their main acquirers. Despite the tremendous superiority of the Saudi armed forces and their partners over virtually any regional adversary in armaments and military equipment, the Saudi-led coalition is demonstrating failure to conduct a protracted military campaign in Yemen.

Although the participation of Middle East states in the processes of political globalization requires the integration of the region, the development of national economies leads to disintegration as such aforementioned. This situation seems to have two main consequences. On the one hand, economic disintegration becomes a factor in increasing intraregional conflict. On the other hand, the imperatives of unity predetermine the especially important role of political (and religious) ideologies that could fulfill the function of consolidation.

Another regional factor concerns demographic dynamics. The socio-economic modernization of the region's societies and the change in the types of population reproduction led to a sharp increase in the population of the countries of the Middle East in the past century. This, of course, is a long-term factor, but its effect has fully become especially noticeable in recent years. Especially, in oil-exporting states where political regimes take increased social obligations, which are emphasized during planting conservative ideologies, minimize motivation to limit birth rates. Population growth, in turn, exacerbated the already existing resource shortage in the Middle East, primarily water. Apparently, a further increase in water scarcity may well become a regional dynamic already in the current century. It can turn into the most important conflict-generating factor.

The perception in the colonial period by the intellectual elites of the region of purely Western philosophical and political teachings and their further adaptation to Arab realities led to the formation of three main currents of social thought, which for decades, having been in sharp confrontation among themselves, about moved various models of independent development through the political parties and movements they created. These were firstly pan-Arabism, or Arab nationalism, secondly Marxism, which drew strength in the existence of the Soviet Union and other socialist states, and lastly Islamism. Each of these movements was transboundary, in fact, transnational in nature, appealing to unifying, integrative slogans. Nationalists saw the future of the region in the creation of a single Arab state, in which all the borders between the Arab territories would be erased. Marxists, in principle, adhered to the concept of the state-nation, but put forward the slogans of class unity, which would underlie the future of their people and their relations with other peoples. Islamists appealed to Muslim unity, putting forward the slogan "Islam is the solution". The balance of power between these three ideological systems was constantly changing. In different periods of the centenary under consideration and in different countries, one of them, then another came to the fore. For example, the Arab Marxists had such a strong influence in Iraq in the 50s of the 20th century and in South Yemen in 1975–1990, but they were pushed back by Arab nationalists. The Arab nationalists were adherents of the three main ideological and political systems. One of them was Nasserism, the ideology and political practice of the Gamal Abdel Nasser regime in Egypt. The other was the Ba'athism (literally meaning "renaissance") in Syria and Iraq. The third one was, finally, the Movement of Arab Nationalists. The Movement of Arab Nationalists was a pan-Arab nationalist organization influential in much of the Arab world, particularly within the Palestinian movement. Even today there are parties belonging to these three political movements, including Nasserists who have separated from the Palestinian fronts, for example, the Democratic Front for the Liberation of Palestine and the Popular Front for the Liberation of Palestine. One of the Ba'athist parties is still the ruling party in Syria. Marxism and Arab nationalism, over time, occupied marginal place in the political landscape. As the Islamists, who created their first political organization, The Muslim Brothers Association, in 1928 in Egypt. It has become an influential force for many years in a number of countries, but defeated by their rivals in the same century. It was legalized during the "Arab spring" and had substantial political power in certain countries (Egypt, Tunisia), as a result of the elections. They even came to power, but they could not keep it. For instance, in 2012 presidential election, its candidate Mohamed Morsi became Egypt's first president to gain power through an election[15]. However, following massive demonstrations and unrest, Morsi was overthrown by the military and placed under house arrest. The group was then banned in Egypt and declared as a terrorist organization[16]. Another example, the Al-Nahda Islamic Party in Tunisia showed flexibility and remained a legitimate political force working with by other parties and not claiming to gain power.

Nevertheless, in the region there are also states formed on the basis of Islamic principles. These are the Islamic Republic of Iran, which arose as a result of the anti-Shah Islamic revolution of 1979, and the Kingdom of Saudi Arabia, which has existed for almost a century and has turned into one of the most influential states in the region over the past decades. But on the one hand, in Iran, elements of a democratic system that are highly developed by regional standards coexist with Islamic principles. On the other hand, in Saudi Arabia, a cautious process has begun, which is still too early to define as "de-Islamization," but which includes overcoming some elements of the archaic and participation in G20 gives respectability to the international status of the country.

The religious component, one way or another, plays an important role in the identity of peoples the vast majority of the Arab states and also to a large extent Israel. Turkey remains the only state constitutionally consolidated secular status at the beginning of the 22th century. It has long been presented as an example of the successful development of the Muslim state in European patterns, but today, she is more inclined towards authoritarianism than de-

---

[15] Hussein Ibish, "Is this the end of the failed Muslim Brotherhood project?", *The National*, 5 October 2013 at https://www.thenational.ae/is-this-the-end-of-the-failed-muslim-brotherhood-project-1.478124, accessed on June 12, 2020.

[16] Nicholas Wade, "Egypt: What poll results reveal about Brotherhood's popularity," BBC News, 30 August 2013 at https://www.bbc.com/news/world-middle-east-23846680, accessed on May 23, 2020.

mocracy and is slowly drifting toward Islamization. It goes, in comparison with Saudi Arabia, paradoxically, in the opposite direction. Moreover, it is easy to notice the consequences for interaction with the outside world, the prospects for Turkey's entry into the EU are becoming increasingly illusive.

Conclusion

As examined in this article, states emerging in the Middle East from the twentieth century to present can be divided into six types. The first of them is Egypt that emerged as a result of national liberation movements in the place of dependent territories. Morocco is the second type of state that has been ruled by Alawite dynasty since the 17th century. Iraq, Syria, Libya, and Kuwait are the third type of states. The formation of such states was usually not easy as their borders were determined by the mother countries at the beginning of the colonial period without taking into account the natural-geographical and demographic realities. The fourth type is states created on the basis of intra-regional expansion or external construction through the migration process. Israel is very important example for this. Palestine has been colonized by Israel since the Jews have returned their lands. In this case, Hebrew was used as tool for the formation of a new national identity and Israel was established as a modern state. The fifth type state in the region is Turkey. Turkey's boundaries are significantly narrowed compared with the four hundred year of Ottoman Era in the region. Turkey, as a successor of the Ottoman Empire, lost most of its territories and was built as a nation state in 1923. The sixth and final state type Iran has maintained the continuity of statehood mainly in historical borders for centuries, but couldn't be transformed into a modern state.

The most important method of state building in the region was political engineering, which was the attempt of the colonial authorities to consciously transfer Western norms, principles, standards, and algorithms in order to functionalize the political system. Otherwise, it was not possible for an external sourced political system to work. The political engineering was carried out by external forces, forcibly and without taking into account local characteristics.

The beginning of the nation-building process in the region caused the Middle East intellectuals to meet the theories of nationalism and the struggle for liberation that emerged after the First World War. In this context, three main approaches have emerged that play an important role in nation building in the Arab world. The first of these, Pan-Arab was based on the idea of linguistic and ethnic unity in the spirit of German nationalism in the 19th century. There were several variations of the Second approach, based on the idea of "country". It appeared before the declaration of statehood in Sudan, Libya and the Gulf monarchy, during the struggle for independence in Egypt, Tunisia and Algeria. Finally, the third approach can be described as Islamic. It was a purely Middle Eastern invention and involved the transformation of Umma (the entire Muslim community associated with Islamic ties) ideas into a nation idea. None of these three approaches has been able to supplant the others for a hundred years of the development of the region.

The early Pan-Arab projects put forward at the beginning of the twentieth century did not extend to the Maghreb countries. However, the formation of the Versailles-Washington system and the emergence of a project of a Jewish national center in Palestine contributed to the gradual formation of a common regional identity, especially in the Arab countries. The Arab-Israeli conflict was central an element of regional relations for half a century. Then Iran has seen as an enemy by a significant part of the Sunni Arab states led by Saudi Arabia. Moreover, rich oil and gas reserves have been found in a number of regional countries. These countries have become key supplier countries in the world energy market. Therefore, they have accumulated significant capital and have used that for military preparations, especially for Israel-Arab (Palestine) Conflict and then Sunni-Shia (Iran) rivalry.

Finally, deep contradictions between different ethnic and religious groups, a lack of historical legitimacy of state borders and territorial disputes, mutual distrust of the elites, etc. created the basis for endless contest for regional leadership. The formation of Israel caused regional conflicts and instability within the region. The religious component, one way or another, plays an important role in the identity of peoples the vast majority of the Arab states and also to a large extent Israel.

www.ingramcontent.com/pod-product-compliance
Lightning Source LLC
LaVergne TN
LVHW040054080526
838202LV00045B/3622